WHAT'S COOKING?

WHAT'S COOKING?

Recipes of a lifetime

MARGUERITE PATTEN

HPL
HAWKER
PUBLICATIONS
LIMITED

First published by
Hawker Publications Ltd
Park House 13
140 Battersea Park Road
London SW11 4NB

Text © 1992 Marguerite Patten
Illustrations © 1992 Hawker Publications Ltd

A CIP catalogue record for this book
is available from the British Library
ISBN 0-9514649-9-X

Illustrator: Kate Simpson
Project editor: Edwina Conner
Assistant editors: Claire Welbourn, Catherine Moore
Designers: Richard Souper, Studio Two
Reproduction: Imposing Images Ltd
Printing and binding: Redwood Press Ltd, Bath

Contents

Preface

To all those who think that being a home economist is dull, and that a career in cookery is even duller, I can only say how wrong they are. I have had an incredibly enjoyable and interesting life. I appreciate that I have been especially fortunate: my work has changed continually over the years and has given me the opportunity to cook and demonstrate in many unusual and exciting places – travelling is a great pleasure to me – and to work with many talented people.

Good cooking undoubtedly depends on the wise choice of foods and using the correct method of blending and heating them; but it is also an *art,* to be cherished and developed. That is why I was so proud to receive the OBE from Her Majesty the Queen for services to the *art* of cookery.

One of the most enjoyable aspects of my work has been meeting the public – all kinds of people with different needs in a wide variety of places. All of us who write about cookery, and give demonstrations in various ways, know that our job is to help people, whatever their talents, to cook successfully for themselves and their families. I believe that enjoyable, nutritious food and happy mealtimes have a very important part to play in our lives.

People often ask me: 'How do you continually think of new ideas and new recipes?' It's not that difficult. I gain constant inspiration from the countries I visit, from the people I meet and from the ever-changing and challenging world of food. This book records many events in my life and the part they have played in teaching me about food and cookery.

Throughout the first part of the book you will find a selection of dishes picked out in **bold type**. The recipes for these dishes can be found in the second half. A few of these recipes date from the years of rationing and austerity – they are part of Britain's history of food – but you will find I have suggested ways in which they may be adapted for today's tastes.

I hope you enjoy cooking these dishes as much as I have done; and that you will find this, the record of a very happy cook, of interest. To my family and the many people who have helped me throughout my life I say a very sincere 'thank you'.

Marguerite Patten
Brighton, 1992

CHAPTER 1

First Course

I am frequently asked if I enjoyed cooking from an early age and the answer is 'No'. I cannot recall any occasions as a little girl when I helped my mother to cook or even had any desire to do so. My great love as I grew up was acting; I dreamed of being a great actress – preferably a Shakespearean one. I only started cooking because I wanted to help my mother, who had to work very hard. When I was 12 and our family were living in High Barnet, Hertfordshire, my father, Wallace Brown, only 38 at the time, died suddenly. He left behind our mother, Elsie, as well as three children, of whom I was the eldest. Philip, my brother, was nearly 10 and our younger sister, Elizabeth, only four. My father's printing business, which turned out wonderful work, was not prosperous, chiefly because he would all too often do things cheaply for 'good friends' and for charities. When all his affairs had been settled it was found he had left no money.

Neither my grandfather, nor my mother's brothers and sisters, all of whom were very supportive at the time, were wealthy. Things looked pretty black for us. My mother had trained as a secondary school teacher, but had given up her career when she married. Luckily, she was a very resourceful woman and within a matter of a few weeks after my father's death she found herself a job as a teacher in a nearby school. There were no vacancies in the senior school at the time, so mother began teaching the smaller children. I remember her coming home after her first day, looking slightly shaken. She had been summoned to the headmistress's study and introduced to a small boy who held a glass eye in his hand. It had come out during some classroom horseplay and the child was unable to put it back. Mother was asked to put it back for him. When she expressed doubts about her ability to perform this operation, the headmistress (who was unmarried) said sharply: 'You are a married woman with children – what's the problem?' To which my poor mother had felt moved to reply: 'The problem is that none of my children have glass eyes!' Nevertheless, she managed to slot the eye back in in its place.

Within a short time she transferred to the senior school, where she remained. Although her life was a busy one I know she loved teaching and found great pleasure in her work with children. Throughout our growing-up years I never remember mother making a fuss about her obvious difficulties in making ends meet. We were very hard up: teachers in those days were badly paid, and women teachers even more so – equal pay was a thing of the future. Even when my mother rose to a senior position in the school, she earned less money than young men considerably her junior in age and responsibility. I know this riled her, for she could be militant about women's rights. I well remember that some months, before the pay cheque arrived, she looked strained and drawn, but she never let her worries spoil our happy life. One month her purse must have been particularly bare, for she had the brilliant idea of feeling down the backs of all the chairs to see if there was buried treasure. To our joy we found quite a few odd pence in the upholstered chairs in the sitting room – a moment of triumph!

When did I first start to cook? I suppose it was when I was nearly 13, and I was on holiday from the grammar school I attended at the time. It was a fee-paying school. While my father was still alive I had taken a scholarship examination – my father believed in finding out just how much his children could achieve. I was not allowed to benefit from this scholarship while my father was living because at that time our income was considered too high. On his death, the head of my school told my mother that I would be awarded the scholarship – a great financial relief to her. At this time we lived in a reasonably comfortable semi-detached house, but one that was very hard work to run, for it seemed full of unnecessary and unwanted stairs. It also had a small garden and I know my mother longed for a much larger one. We had to wait until I was nearly 20 before mother could buy a modern house with a garden sufficiently large to grow as much in the way of fruit and vegetables as she wanted. She was a real country woman at heart.

Meanwhile, with her working day, we children to care and cook for, and a house that had to be cleaned, my mother needed help. My holidays were longer than those of the school where she taught, so when she was at work and I was at home I decided I would cook the family lunch. In those days school meals were unknown – they were brought in as a wartime measure. Pupils went home for the lunch break of two hours.

I started off with an ambitious dish: rabbit pie. At that time rabbit was a favourite food in Britain. I started making the pastry and the pie filling after breakfast, following the instructions in a cookery book. I had nearly finished when a school friend arrived. I don't know why I started showing off so badly, but I balanced the pie on the palm of one hand – held high in the air – while I cut away the surplus pastry. This was all too much for my friend. She gave my hand a flip to deflate my foolish pride – and there

9

was the pie upside down on the floor! I would like to report that, in a hygienic manner, I discarded the food. But that would have meant no lunch. So I humbly confess that I gathered up the bits and somehow put them together again. Perhaps luckily I have no recollection of how the pie tasted! The recipe for **Chicken Pie** can also be made with rabbit.

I have included this particular recipe, an adaptation of a traditional West Country dish, as a link with Bath, where I was born in November, 1915, and where we lived until moving to High Barnet when I was nearly five years old. I heard my mother describe this dish on several occasions, although I never remember her making it. It was a speciality of my father's mother, an enthusiastic and clever cook, who delighted in entertaining her friends. I wish I could remember her but she died quite suddenly when I was very young.

Bath was my father's home, where he was born and grew up. He worked for a time in the Forest of Dean in Gloucestershire, and that is where he met my mother, who was teaching in that area. After their marriage, in 1914, just before war broke out, they moved to Bath. My father became the manager of a large printing business. He worked there for a time before serving in he army. During the war he was severely gassed – he was blinded for a time – and, although he recovered after several years, the experience was gruelling for both my parents and grandparents. I know my mother was grateful for the affection and support of her mother-in-law at this time, for she knew relatively few people in Bath. My grandmother must have been a very special person.

When my father recovered his sight, he was told by his doctors that he had to work out of doors for a year or so if he wanted to recover properly. So my parents bought a dairy business in Bath and, as a child, I loved to hear my mother describe the problems they had with the mule that drew the dairy cart. It sounded fun to me, but I know they both hated this period and were thankful when my father had recovered from the gas sufficiently to return to printing. We moved to Barnet, where my father purchased an existing printing business.

My father was not only an expert printer but an incredibly gifted pianist. At some period of his life he received lessons on the organ too, and had had the opportunity to play the the organ in Bath Abbey. He was a great stalwart of the British Legion and frequently played at charity concerts to support them and many other causes. Unfortunately he often agreed to teach the piano to the children of various friends in Barnet – quite free. He would give the child one or two lessons, realise there was little talent there and abandon them, saying to my mother: 'You can take them on'. Mother was a reasonably competent pianist but certainly did not want this extra task. Like most girls of that era I had piano lessons, not from either parent, but from an outside teacher who came to our house. The whole family would pray my lesson would end before my father came home as his opinion of my teacher's ability and mine were not exactly flattering. Although I have no talent for playing the piano, I have a great love of music and my father's affection for appearing on a platform has been handed down to me.

My unfortunate experience with the rabbit pie did not prevent my carrying on with the cooking, and I began to enjoy the job very much indeed. I learned a lot from mother about making economical food interesting – we loved her **Cheesey Potatoes** (a modest form of soufflé); her steak and kidney pudding (she always made enough for two meals); and her lovely way of cooking a lamb stew so it had a slightly caramel taste. I learned years later that this was a technique used in **Navarin of Lamb**. Her salads were much more adventurous than the more ordinary variety common at the time and I felt embarrassed when people exclaimed at the sight of black or redcurrants, raspberries or other fruits nestling between the familiar lettuce and watercress. Why couldn't our salads look like everyone else's? I now know that using fruit from the garden saved money and also produced salads of excellent flavour, completely in keeping with today's ideas. You will find some of these under **Mother's Salads**. Her bread and butter pudding was a popular dessert: how surprised she would have been to find it was considered a gourmet dish in the 1990s.

I learned several important lessons from my mother. The first was how to make economical food interesting – **Crunchy Herrings, Surprise Toad in the Hole** and her lovely lovely stuffed vegetables and vegetable soups demonstrated this skill perfectly. Then there was planning ahead – an essential talent for working women. And although Mother would be the first to say she did not shine at making cakes, we did love her **Suffolk Rusks** – dating from her childhood days in that county – and her fresh **Cobs** straight from the oven. Her sponges on the other hand were a source of frustration for her and fun for us children. The results would vary between a thin, crunchy, biscuit-like confection and a cake that puffed-up in a truly dramatic style. I think she was glad when I took over cake-making. We had a local café where we went some Saturday mornings after shopping and their **Maids of Honour** were some of the best I have ever tasted. That's when I discovered the pleasure of experimenting. I tried a number of times to make Maids of Honour that looked and tasted just like those we had in the café – what a feeling of triumph when the family agreed I had succeeded.

As children we had few fads in the way of food, which was a good thing, for I am sure some of my early experiments were a trifle odd. Philip had one dislike – blancmange, a popular dessert of that era. I decided that it was the name he objected to, so I put my imagination to work, added some dried fruits to the hot milk, decorated the finished dish so that it was unrecognisable, and presented it. No fool my brother, he could recognise blancmange underneath any disguise!

I know brothers and sisters are supposed to quarrel wildly, not only as children, but throughout their lives. It sounds horribly smug, but although, of course, we did argue when we were young, there have never been any serious differences between us. I always say that it was impossible to quarrel with Philip because he was always so calm and placid. I am sure this aspect of his personality was of great value when he became a ship's officer and later a Trinity House pilot (a sea pilot). Philip gets results in a very quiet, positive way. When Philip says 'No', he means it.

Elizabeth was our pride and joy when she was a little girl. I think Philip and I felt like extra parents as we were some years older than she was. She was always more academically inclined than we were, although Philip had plenty of tough exams at various stages of his career in the merchant navy.

Elizabeth was, as the future showed, a born teacher, just like our mother.

As children, we were all lucky to have happy holidays with various relatives, all of whom seemed to live in interesting parts of Britain.

It was during our growing-up years that we spent time with an aunt in the Forest of Dean, Gloucestershire – surely one of the most beautiful parts of Britain. I developed a liking for all kinds of different foods. Many country people kept a pig in those days. I enjoyed the chitterlings – hence my love of the French *andouilletes* – pigs trotters and home-made brawn. Aunt, and various cousins, prepared salmon – caught in the river Wye – as a special treat for us. **Salmon in a Crust** is known as salmon *en croûte* nowadays. The dish we called **Itsy-Bitsy Salmon** is a lovely way of using the small pieces of leftover fish.

Our grandfather remained in Bath, where I was born. I loved to go there and stay with him and our step-grandmother. My grandfather had remarried after my grandmother died. My step-grandmother was also a good cook; her recipe for **Easter Biscuits** is worth remembering. We had these rich currant shortbreads at Eastertime – hence the name; but they are good throughout the year.

The only drawback about visiting Bath was my grandfather's belief in the medicinal value of the spa water there: we would be taken to the Pump Room to drink this horrid warm liquid. Several times I was put on the train clutching a large bottle of this water to take home to mother – as a special treat for her, and a reminder of her early days of marriage. Fortunately, mother had less strong feelings about the taste of the water than I did, and duly drank it. As I got older, I hated carrying this bottle and I'm sorry to say that once or twice the contents were tipped down the train's toilet.

Domestic science was of little importance at the school I attended. It had a good academic standing and I suppose I was an average scholar. The school had a splendid record in games, which I disliked and at which I was a complete duffer. One day, when netball had to be abandoned due to the wet, the games mistress fixed me with a steely gaze and said, 'You're glad it's raining, aren't you?' to which I had to reply, 'Yes'.

There was an occasion when we had one or two cookery lessons; I think it was towards the end of a term, after exams. My only memory was of having to measure pieces of rhubarb, to make sure they were absolutely the same length and, when they were cooked, to arrange the drooping pieces in a cut-glass bowl. Hardly inspiring – or *cordon bleu* cookery!

The question soon arose as to what I was going to do when I left school. I came from a family where most of the girls had been trained as teachers. Having tasted my culinary efforts, my aunts and uncles outlined the joys of being a domestic science teacher – the term home economist was never used then. But I was absolutely determined I was *not going to teach*. I declared I would hate it. (In view of the many hours I spent lecturing in colleges in later years – and loving every minute of the time – that decision was really rather amusing.) My ambition was still to go on the stage, but that seemed impossible. My mother tried to encourage me to stay at school after matriculation year to take Higher School Certificate (the forerunner of A levels); she felt the extra two years would give me time to decide more wisely about my future. I wouldn't do that either. Even stronger than my desire to go on the stage was my burning ambition to get to work and earn some money to help mother. Both my brother and sister felt the same when they got older.

I left school and for a year took various odd office jobs to make money, but had the sense to attend evening classes in cookery. As well as learning practical skills, I learned something of the theory behind cooking.

A friend of my mother's told her that women were being employed the gas and electricity industries as advisers and suggested that it could be a way for me to combine my liking for cooking with the chance to stand on a platform and demonstrate – a way of performing. It sounded interesting, so I started to apply for jobs.

At the same time I worked hard to equip myself to take the entrance exam for the Royal Academy of Dramatic Art – just to see if I *could* act. Although I had left school, one of the English mistresses helped me select my 'party pieces' for the audition and gave up time to rehearse me. The day came for the examination in London. Although everyone at RADA was most friendly, it was a nerve-wracking occasion. I was not given any clue at the time as to how well, or badly, I had fared. I had to wait for a letter. This finally came announcing that I *had* been awarded a place. Alas, I knew I couldn't accept it: there were no grants for studying acting. But at least I had proved to myself that I *could* have done it.

At this stage I was offered a good job with the Barnet branch of the Northern Metropolitan Electricity Supply Company, officially known as the Northmet. I decided to take it and use every opportunity to take part in local amateur dramatics.

CHAPTER 2

The Cook and the Showgirl

T he year was 1933, and I was 18 years old. The electricity industry had not yet been nationalized and there was a great difference in the size, and efficiency, of the firms and local authorities which supplied electricity. When I started to travel around Britain several years later, I realised how lucky I had been to start my career in such a progressive firm as the Northmet and to work under Enid Yetton, a wonderfully encouraging person. I am so glad that I have been able to record my gratitude to her on a number of occasions.

From the moment I started at the Northmet I was encouraged to go to various Polytechnics for courses in nutrition, fabric care and home laundry work and extra cookery. (I think it would be fair to say that I was 'pushed' into going!) We young home economists also had lessons in cake-making from the Miss Scotts, two sisters who ran an excellent home-made bakery business. This was a very important part of my education, for in those days the audiences at a demonstration were served a most lavish tea or, if they came to an evening demonstration, given savoury foods.

There was quite a team of us, and when it was our turn to prepare the food for these occasions we all tried to out-do our colleagues. It was small wonder that the demonstrations were so well attended!

What kind of food did we prepare? I think this list will remind anyone old enough to remember of the glories of pre-war teatime. Various scones, including drop scones (Scotch pancakes), were a necessity. In those days electric cookers had large oblong grill-boilers and solid hotplates, and these were perfect for cooking drop scones. We always made a large sponge and a fruit cake, to demonstrate the even baking of the electric oven. There would be plates of buttered tea-breads, such as **Apricot and Walnut Loaf**, **Coconut Pyramids**, **Frangipane and Macaroon Tartlets**, also coconut-coated **Madeleines**. We served pyramids of **Meringues** and crisp biscuits such as **Melting Moments** and **Florentines**. Our savoury dishes would include miniature sausage-rolls, vol-au-vents and cheese savouries. There was no frozen puff pastry in those days, so the pastry had to be home-made.

Enid Yetton made sure that we youngsters were never pushed forward too quickly: we progressed steadily, learning as we went along. We learned how to deal with the public and attend to their needs. As a junior home economist (home economists were known as demonstrators at the time) my job was to prepare the basic ingredients for the seniors – I weighed out the ingredients, checked that all utensils were available and assisted during the demonstration. I might do a little beating or stirring once or twice during the session, or perhaps add the garnish to a dish. The ability to assist at a demonstration is a real talent. So much of the success of the presentation depends on co-operation between the demonstrator and his, or her, assistant. It's rather like a hospital operation where instruments have to be available instantly to the surgeon.

A big part of our job was to offer a service to members of the public purchasing electrical appliances. When someone bought a new electric cooker, for instance, one of us would visit that person's home and show them how it should be used. If required to do so, we would cook a dish, or even a meal. Sometimes we were imposed upon by the public. I well remember one occasion when a woman purchased a cooker, asked for someone to go and explain how to use it and do some cooking. She was not available during the daytime so this had to be an evening visit. Off I went and discovered that my task was to cook a complete 5-course dinner-party meal for six people, dish-up each course and then clear up the kitchen. I think that might be described as service with a capital 'S'!

We also undertook to show people how to use new washing machines and the large rotary-type ironers that had made their appearance as a domestic appliance. Now and again we were expected to do a week's family wash to demonstrate the machine, and often iron several shirts.

I gave my first cookery demonstration sooner than I expected. This was a lucky break because it meant I progressed more quickly than I otherwise might have done. But at the time I was scared stiff and felt it was bad rather than good luck! The senior I was supposed to assist one day was suddenly taken ill. Everyone else had engagements for the day, and I was the only person left to give the demonstration. This particular senior home economist was a beautiful pastry cook and she had planned a demonstration that included cakes and pastries. The programme had been advertised, so I had to follow it. Off I went, my knees trembling, to give my first demonstration at Potters Bar, near Barnet.

It was a charming demonstration room that did not take a large number of people, so my first audience was a small one. In the morning I made my preparations, cooked the cakes for tea and checked all the recipe ingredients – so far so good. I was ready for the fray.

The first thing I made was choux pastry and I piped the mixture on to the trays for **Choux Buns.** When they came out of the oven they looked

magnificent – my audience applauded. Sadly, pride comes before a fall! It was a beautifully sunny day, the windows were open and I put the buns on their cooking trays by the open window. Experienced cooks will realise my folly. I had not checked that these were quite crisp and I cooled them in a draught – a fatal mistake. When I came to fill them later I was left with miserable, flat objects. I had been so busy cooking other dishes that I had ignored the choux buns. It was many, many years before I would include any form of choux pastry in a demonstration!

Almost immediately after this I had to step in to give a demonstration in a large hall. I suppose I was nearly ready for this stage in my career and these sudden emergencies gave me the chance to show what I could do. From then onwards I took on more and more demonstrations.

The electrical industry held a yearly public speaking contest and the Northmet had their own finals. In 1936 I won the local heat and came second in the contest for the whole country. I felt this was very much due to the acting I was doing at the time. I had joined a local amateur dramatic group, organised by a lecturer from the Guildhall School of Music, London, and in the summer of 1936 I also had a working holiday at the Little Theatre, Bath. This was organized by a charming couple, Peter and Consuela King. I was able to stay with my grandfather, who was not certain if he approved of these theatrical affairs, but was always delighted to see any of his grandchildren. My time at Bath was a delight. Consuela was a large, efficient lady, a great organizer, and Peter was an expert on voice production and make-up. It was from him that I learned how to adapt my voice if I had a bad cold and had to perform in public. I have often been grateful for his advice.

The Kings also ran weekend courses at the Everyman Theatre, Hampstead, which were attended by amateurs and young professionals. I attended, and this set the scene for the next step in my life. I became very friendly with a young professional actress who was 'resting' between jobs. Suddenly she had the offer of two jobs from different repertory companies, one at the Theatre Royal, Oldham, the other in Bristol. She accepted the place at Bristol and said to Oldham: 'My friend Marguerite could come to you'.

What a panic! Her letter of explanation to me and a letter from the Theatre Royal, Oldham arrived the same morning. What should I do? I had a good career which was becoming more and more interesting, but this was such a good opportunity to act. As usual, I turned to my mother for advice. 'Go', she said, 'if you don't, you'll be wondering all your life if you could have made the grade on the professional stage'. Obviously I had to advise the Northmet. The manager was practical and helpful. 'You have nothing to lose,' he pointed out, 'your holiday is due, and they're only asking you to go for three weeks on trial; if you fail we shall be pleased to have you back. If you are successful then it is up to you to decide what to do.' Many friends thought me very foolish to consider changing my way of life, but nevertheless off to Oldham I went.

CHAPTER 3

A Developing Talent

Like many people who are born and live in the south of England I had no real knowledge about the northern part of the country. Friends, who knew as little about it as I did, painted a gloomy picture of dirt and industrial haze. So I was surprised to find that Oldham was a pleasant industrial town and, as it was early summer and the weather was good, it looked its best.

I travelled to Oldham on a Thursday in June, 1937, and stayed at a local small hotel. On the Friday morning, I went to the theatre to meet the producer of the company. His name was Arthur Leslie, who of course later became very well known as the first landlord of the 'Rover's Return' in the TV series, *Coronation Street*. He was busy rehearsing the next week's performance but stopped to introduce me to the other members of the company, who all made me feel welcome. Joan, a young actress, told me there was a spare room at the house where she lodged and we arranged that I should take it. My new friend, also suggested that I spend the Sunday with her family, who lived just outside Manchester. That short journey gave me my first brief look at the lovely countryside so near to all towns in Lancashire.

I was lucky to be in this company. Arthur, who played leading male roles, and his wife, Betty, also an actress, were delightful people, always anxious to make sure that we younger members of the company were happy.

On the Monday I started rehearsing for the following week's production, in which I had a sizeable part. I was not working nearly as hard as fellow members of the company, for I had only one part to learn and most of them had two. In those days before television began, a theatre offering twice-nightly repertory could be found in most good-sized towns. In Oldham there were two theatres, but only one, the Oldham Coliseum, survives today. If it sounds as if working in repertory was an easy life, let me correct this impression. It was incredibly hard work. Every evening there were two performances of the current play and every morning we rehearsed the next week's play. The first read through started on the Monday morning. Here we walked through the move-ments – with virtually no props. During the week we had to become word-perfect, and plan what to wear on stage. For my very first week's role I had to produce a tennis outfit, so a hasty SOS went home to ask if I could borrow this from a tennis-playing friend. In another scene I had to wear a wedding dress. As I had nothing suitable in my wardrobe, the easiest and cheapest thing was to make it. I bought the material and sewed industriously during the afternoons. Fortunately, I was used to making my own clothes – most people sewed in those days. I don't think I'd have won any prizes for beautiful stitching, but the general effect was satisfactory.

After three weeks on probation I was asked to become one of the company, playing a variety of parts in the popular plays of that time. I had no qualms about accepting: I was simply enjoying myself too much to go back to the Northmet.

The audiences were enthusiastic, but highly critical. If any of us were inaudible in the gallery – where the seats cost the princely sum of 4d (1.5p) – we would hear a shout: 'Speak up luv!' And if the occasion warranted it, they were quick to hand out good advice. In one play I was the innocent victim. The murderer was creeping up behind me. At every performance I would be warned by at least one loud voice from the audience: 'Look out luv – he's behind you!'

The months passed by very quickly, and happily. On Sundays, if the weather was good, we would try and get into the country to breathe fresh air and rehearse our parts. We also rehearsed last thing at night before going to bed. That was the good thing about sharing lodgings with a fellow actress, we could hear each other's lines. I had heard that if you rehearsed last thing at night you would remember the words the next morning very clearly. I don't know if this was true for everyone, but it certainly worked for me. I still use this technique today; whenever I have a presentation or demonstration of any kind, I invariably go through what I have to say just before going to sleep.

I learned a little about cooking in Lancashire during that period. My landlady would cook any food we chose to buy, or would provide us with family fare and charge us accordingly. I tasted black pudding, faggots and pease pudding and home-made Eccles cakes, all of which were delicious.

I had been in Oldham for six months. It was now nearly Christmas, 1937, and the season was ending for Arthur's company: the theatre was to be used by entirely different actors for the pantomime season. We all hoped that we would meet up again when we the company opened in Leicester the following April, but there was no certainty of that. Obviously we all had to try and find jobs before that.

After a happy Christmas at home it was time to think about a new job. My brother was a cadet in the Merchant Navy and my sister still at school, so I had no intention of 'resting' – to use the stage parlance.

I consulted my late chief at the Northmet and she advised writing round to various firms to try and get a job selling refrigerators. In 1938 these were beginning to gain importance. So I wrote off to Frigidaire. It is strange to think that this company – whose name was once a generic term – is no more. I still remember the old rhyme: 'When baby's screams get hard to bear/Put him in the Frigidaire!'

I was surprised, but delighted, when a letter arrived by return of post, asking me to go for an interview. Fate took a hand in my affairs at this point. My letter, asking to be a run-of-the-mill saleswoman, had arrived at a time when Frigidaire had advertised for a senior home economist. When I arrived at the appointed time, I was amazed to find so many women waiting to be interviewed. They were all hoping to get this more important position. It's strange, isn't it, that when we are presented with a challenge we somehow find the strength to rise to it. When I was interviewed, I forgot all about being a temporary saleswoman and did my utmost to get this better job. I was sure I had no chance – everyone else seemed more experienced than I was. Much to my surprise I was asked to wait with three or four other candidates for second interviews. After that we were all seen together. It was obviously a close contest.

One of the interviewers was American – Frigidaire belonged to General Motors of the USA. I can still hear that pleasant American drawl saying, 'Well, there's only one way to find out which of you is the best demonstrator: give us a 10-minute demonstration on using a Frigidaire'.

There was *no* refrigerator, *no* table, *no* equipment, but remember I had experienced some weeks rehearsing a play in similar circumstances. You might say I had an unfair advantage. I got the job. The salary made me gasp, it was so generous, and I was told I was expected to travel everywhere first-class and to stay in the very best hotels, to uphold Frigidaire's quality image. I went home in a daze. When I recovered, I decided to take this unbelievable job, do it to the best of my ability for a few months, and then leave when I could return to the stage.

I reported for duty about a week later and my immediate superior handed me a letter saying, 'There's your first important assignment.' I looked at it and almost turned tail and ran. Frigidaire's home economist was to give a full morning's lecture on refrigeration and the art of demonstrating dishes suitable for the refrigerator – a new concept at the time – at a conference attended by most of the senior home economists in the electrical industry. I knew that the technical experts of Frigidaire would brief me well, but how dare I give advice on refrigerator dishes to people who were so much more experienced than I?

Once again I looked around for help. The Electrical Association for Women had a wonderful home economist, whom I had met and regarded with great admiration and awe. She was briskly reassuring. 'Don't worry, you may not know much about refrigerator dishes, but nor does anyone else in Britain at the moment. All you have to do is to be one step ahead of them.' We pored over American magazines and I experimented at home, so I had practical, as well as theoretical experience, of the dishes. I also went around the factory, gathering information about technical data. I had just over two weeks to prepare my material and I'm happy to report that my hard work paid off: the lecture went well.

From then on I travelled around Britain giving demonstrations to the public. It may sound odd to call a demonstration 'Cold Cookery' but that was the name given to the dishes used to demonstrate the advantages of owning a refrigerator. I made several kinds of **Ice Creams** and **Sorbets** and always a mousse of some kind, to show the speed of setting a jellied mixture. The **Maraschino and Apricot Mousse** is still a favourite, although today I may well use lower fat yoghurt rather than double cream. The audience was offered iced coffee and other cold drinks. This was an innovation because at that time Britain had the reputation of serving drinks, including beer, lukewarm in summertime.

Salads of various kinds were included and I was grateful for my mother's good ideas on this subject. Invariably I showed dishes that used leftovers in inspiring ways, for one of the advantages of owning a refrigerator was being able to store these safely for later use. It must sound strange today, when we accept refrigerators as an essential appliance, but I had to work hard to persuade people that they were useful. Relatively few homes had a refrigerator. In a manual of the time people were urged *not* to switch their refrigerator off in winter.

When the time came to consider leaving I realised how foolish I would be. I had no guarantee that I would be successful on the stage, I had a splendid job – why change? I had returned to the weekend courses at the Everyman Theatre, so my urge to act a number of challenging roles was being satisfied. We were excited at the possibility of putting on a satirical play based on *Alice in Wonderland* with Hitler and Mussolini as Tweedle-Dum and Tweedle-Dee – I was playing Alice. There was talk that this could go on to the professional stage but because of the war it never happened.

As the summer of 1939 approached it was obvious that war was imminent and that refrigerator demonstrations were to be a thing of the past. I had to find another job.

I was quite ready to do something entirely different. I was offered a post as an area supervisor of hostels for the Land Army. A few years later I had an opportunity to appreciate just how hard the Land Girls worked; my sister worked in the Land Army for a time, before going to college to train as a teacher. Unfortunately, I couldn't accept this post, for it meant driving a car and I had not yet learned to drive. I accepted a post as a home economist with the Yorkshire, North Lincolnshire and Howdenshire Electricity Co Ltd, which covered parts of Lincolnshire and Yorkshire. I was due to start work in Bradford at the beginning of September, 1939. I had misgivings about being away from home but, like everyone, hoped that a miracle would happen and war would be averted.

Before I took the job, my mother, sister and I had a lovely holiday in Wimereaux, a small seaside resort near Boulogne, France. For the first time I tasted *escargots*, frog's legs and some other classic French fish dishes. I was surprised at the mild flavour of frog's legs – to my palate they tasted like a blend of chicken and salmon. Our little hotel overlooked the town square and church. It was sobering to see the stream of young French soldiers going in there each day. It brought the prospect of war very near. When we returned home, towards the end of August, the ship was packed with people, many of whom had shortened their holidays to be sure they were back in Britain *if* the worst happened.

CHAPTER 4

The Kitchen Front

It was a particularly beautiful day when I awoke in my room in Bradford on 3 September, 1939, and the sun was streaming in through the windows. The landlady, when she brought in my breakfast, talked about everything but the one thing that was on everyone's minds – the possibility of war.

I'm sure everyone remembers where they were when Neville Chamberlain announced that we were at war with Germany. Somehow the the Prime Minister's calm tone made it sound even more frightening than if he had shouted the news at the top of his voice. I joined a fellow tenant for coffee and we listened to the radio together. I was very grateful not to be alone at such a time. Here I sat, 24 years old, feeling I was part of a strange new world where I knew no one.

As the speech ended, this new acquaintance and I sat quietly. We could think of nothing to say. I'm sure many people all over the country reacted in the same way. Later we lunched together and discussed our plans. My instinct was to pack my bags and catch the next train home to be with my mother and sister. (My brother was now an officer in the merchant navy and was at sea across the other side of the world.) But the manager of the electricity company and my mother both urged me to stay put and see what happened. So I decided that unless things became very grim in and around London, Bradford would be my home for the next months.

Everyone at my new job was very friendly and soon one of my colleagues adopted me and I enjoyed happy Sunday afternoons at her home in the country just outside Bradford. This was particularly welcome, for Saturdays were extremely busy. We worked all day and I also offered to be one of the cooks at an all-night ARP canteen which was run at Police Headquarters. This was pretty hectic with policemen and ARP workers all rushing in for their food. Rationing was not yet in force and I have never fried so many chips, eggs, sausages and bacon rashers in my life. There were endless large cups of strong tea and mountains of toast and butter too. There was no quarter given – even if you were a volunteer. 'Come on miss, make it snappy,' would be the cry, as I struggled to serve everyone as quickly as I could. At 5am every Sunday morning the police drove me home, where I fell into bed for a few hours' sleep.

I stayed in Bradford until the end of 1939 and was then asked to take charge of the company's branch in Lincoln. Although I was sorry to leave my friends behind, I looked forward to this new experience. As it happens, the move to Lincoln shaped my future life, for it was here that I met my husband.

My first job was to find somewhere to live. Accommodation was scarce in a city where there were so many Air Force personnel, as their families had taken all the vacant rooms. Then my mother heard through friends of a certain Vera Hickmott who lived at Waddington, a village just outside Lincoln. Her husband was away on war work, and she wanted someone to share her house. I moved in.

I soon settled down in Lincoln. It was an interesting city, and Waddington, like most villages, had a busy community life. I made friends quickly and started to work in the evenings with the Education Authority giving cookery demonstrations on wartime cookery. We also gave these in the company's demonstration theatre, where the facilities were excellent, but unfortunately the cookers and working facilities in some of the aged village halls around Lincoln were far from perfect. One memorable evening was spent surveying my audience with the tears pouring down my face – and they were weeping too. No, we hadn't experienced a tragedy –

the oil stove, on which I had to cook, hadn't been used in years. The caretaker assured me it would be all right in time – but time was not on my side! Throughout the evening the room was enveloped in oil fumes.

Once rationing began, in January 1940, it was my job to encourage people to adjust their familiar menus. At this stage of the war, special wartime recipes had not yet been developed. Stews now had to be made with the minimum of meat and the maximum of vegetables; chops and steaks were half their usual size; cakes and puddings made with half the standard amounts of fat and sugar. And cream? Oh, that was a thing of the past. It had to be used to make butter and cheese which were considered essentials. The farming communities, with whom I came into contact when demonstrating outside Lincoln, were luckier than most people. They kept chickens and sometimes pigs – although there were strict rules governing how many of the eggs and how much pork or bacon they could keep for themselves. They probably caught rabbits and game birds too – all of which were unknown to town dwellers. On the other hand, rationing was harder on these people, than on town dwellers who had always had to be careful about their food bills. (Details of the weekly ration can be found on p.31.)

We were fortunate to escape the various raids that were beginning to be part of life in towns and cities throughout Britain; but one night an enemy land mine was dropped on Waddington. Fortunately, like so many of the villages in that part of the world, the village boasted a very large church, quite out of proportion to the number of houses; and it was the church – thankfully empty at the time – that bore the brunt of the explosion. Not one person was killed, but almost every house near it, with the exception of ours, was badly damaged. Up to that time there had been just two of us living in a fairly big house. Now, suddenly, we were full to overflowing. A squadron commander and his wife and baby son moved in, followed by another RAF couple. Their houses were uninhabitable.

After that, our lives changed a lot, for both my friend and I were very much involved with the RAF station at Waddington. We met so many of the flying crews. We were entertained by them in the mess and fed them at home as best we could. What did we give them? Mostly vegetable dishes – adorned by microscopic pieces of meat. We could sometimes get sausages, if our butcher had supplies. Fish was particularly difficult to obtain away from the coast. We had a splendid local baker who baked at night, and we used to buy fresh loaves late in the evening and snack on 'bits and pieces' (anything we had available) on squares of doughy hot bread. We were great consumers of soup during those years. There was nothing like a steaming bowlful to keep you awake on fire-watching duty or for comfort during an air raid. Two of my favourite soups of that period were a pleasant **Bortsch** and a satisfying **Oatmeal Soup**.

The more festive occasions took place between hard work because, like most people, I was fire-watching at least one night a week. Men were being called up so those left had to do the job of two or more. I was put in charge of the electricians in the absence elsewhere of the true manager, who was then responsible for a huge area. I humbly confess that I am a very untechnical person. I was sent on a course to learn how to repair electrical appliances but what a blessing that I never needed to use this information, for I fear washing machines, cookers and refrigerators may never have worked again! I have always wanted to meet the foreman electrician at Lincoln again to convey my thanks to him. Never have I known a more tactful person. While I was acting manager, he would come to discuss the day's work with me and ask me technical questions in such a way that I always gave the right answers – what an asset to the Diplomatic Service he would have been.

If it sounds as though life was great fun in those days, I am giving an incomplete impression. There were good times, yes, but there were many sad days too. It was common to meet a young man one day, perhaps dance with him in the mess, or join him for a drink and find that the next day he had been killed. Bomber Command had a terrible toll of tragedies.

The women in our house used to listen to the heavy drone of the Lancasters flying out at night on a raid, and try to gauge the number. None of us slept well, for we were listening for the welcome sound of the planes returning to base. The first person awake roused the rest of the household and we would count the planes as they returned – all too often there were far fewer coming back than flying out. That period was a nightmare for anyone who had someone they cared for in the services.

When I first met Bob at Waddington at the beginning of 1942, he was on what was called the Conversion Flight, for flying crews were converting from Manchesters, the twin-engined version of the Lancaster bomber to the famous Lancasters. Bob was a gunnery officer and his first flight in a Lancaster in January, 1942, was with Squadron Leader John Nettleton, VC, who, sadly, was one of the many, many people in the RAF killed during the war.

Bob had experienced a very eventful service life up to then. He volunteered for the RAF when war was imminent, was given a commission and sent out to Habbaniya in Iraq to train as a gunner. He flew Wellingtons on many bombing operations in the Western desert. Then one day at the end of April 1941, his plane crashed in an Arab graveyard in the middle of the desert. Two of the crew were killed, another was seriously injured, but Bob and a fellow crew member were able to get him out of the wrecked plane. For 48 hours they walked through the desert to try and get help. They were fortunate enough to be picked up by the 10th Hussars regiment and found that if they had walked in the opposite direction they would have met the German army and spent the next years in a prisoner of war camp. The injured crewman was found and saved.

Bob was brought home by ship via South Africa and Canada, a somewhat circuitous route, but very necessary since it was too dangerous to bring ships through the Mediterranean. Bob and I were extremely fortunate, for Bob survived two tours of operations from Britain plus many, many more in the Western desert, making over 80 raids in all; and two further air crashes! I call him 'Bob' and so do most people but his real name is Charles Alfred Patten. I am proud of my OBE, but still more of Bob's awards, for he holds the MBE and the DFC.

There was one party in Lincoln I shall always remember. It was a lovely evening, the windows were open, music was playing and quite a crowd of us were dancing. Suddenly we stopped – the church bells were ringing! Nothing strange in that you may think, but on the outbreak of war it was decreed that the bells would only ring to signify a German invasion. It had come! Someone said to me, 'Can you shoot?' and thrust a revolver into my shaking hand; fortunately, even before I had my first lesson in marksmanship, we learned it was a false alarm.

Bob and I were married in 1942. It was an eventful year for me, because I also decided to accept an offer to join the Ministry of Food. My work in the electrical industry could not be regarded as essential war work and I hoped my experience of giving cookery demonstrations for a number of years might be a useful asset in my new, more useful, position.

I was interviewed in London by several senior members of the Food Advice Division of the Ministry of Food. Before this I knew virtually nothing about the work being carried out by this particular department. I learned that this section of the Ministry had been enlarged and its job was to give the maximum help and advice to the public by means of demonstrations, lectures and informal meetings, as well as printed leaflets, pamphlets and press notices. It was essential that everyone in the country made the very best use of both the rationed, and unrationed, foods available, so that they, and their families, were adequately fed and therefore maintained good health. Centres had been established throughout Britain, staffed by teams of home economists from industry or education, and by dieticians. Each team was headed by an organizer and senior adviser.

I was duly appointed senior adviser in the East Anglia area and I was to be based in Cambridge, the centre for the area.That was certainly a disappointment. I looked forward to the work but I had hoped I could live near Lincoln so that I could be with Bob or, failing that, to have a London appointment, so that I could live with my mother in Barnet.

Neither was possible – there were no vacancies in either area. And I also knew that they needed someone in Cambridge who was used to demonstrating to adults, as the rest of the team, although very experienced, had worked mainly with children.

I arrived in Cambridge on the Sunday, found somewhere to live and toured the city. I peered through the window of the centre and saw that it was equipped with cookers and chairs. Hooray! Back to demonstrations.

On the Monday morning I met my future colleagues. This was the only time of the week when we were likely to be together, for the East Anglia area was a large one, and we all had to travel a good deal – not easy in wartime when public transport was so restricted. The team I was to work with were all very pleasant, although the organiser, Winifred Hargreaves was alarming. She radiated efficiency but had an incredibly brusque manner. I never feel guilty about describing her in this way, because in a very short time we became good friends and I realised that she was one of the kindest and most considerate people I had ever met. At first acquaintance though she *was* pretty terrifying!

Years later, when I began visiting training colleges, to give lectures to young home economists, I found Winifred's name worked like a charm. If, as occasionally happened at our first meeting, one or two senior lecturers were a trifle uppish I would say, 'I'm sure you know my good friend, Miss Hargreaves?' By this time Winifred was very grand. She had become HM Staff Inspector of Home Economics with the Ministry of Education. It worked like a charm: I was immediately treated with great respect. If I knew Miss Hargreaves, I must have *some* value!

I spent my first day in Cambridge finding out about the activities already planned. As well as regular cookery demonstrations in the centre, there were to be others in department stores, and talks in the lunchtime and evening breaks to workers in local factory canteens (factories were working day and night in wartime). There were visits to the outpatient departments of hospitals in the area as well as to Welfare Clinics. (Expectant mothers, babies and young children had extra needs, so they were allowed additional rations, including more milk and bottled orange juice, and it was important they knew about these.) I began to realise just what was entailed in working for the Ministry of Food. We couldn't wait for the public to come to us for advice; we had to go out and meet them.

Towards the end of that first day Winifred Hargreaves said, 'You will

have to make an early start in the morning, to get the stall in position'.
'The stall?' I queried. 'Yes, in the market,' was the reply. 'I have never
demonstrated behind a market stall before,' I announced, in what I
hoped was a suitably dignified manner, worthy of a senior home
economist. I have no doubt that I sounded both pompous and childish.
'Well, now's your chance,' I was told brusquely. How richly I deserved that
uncompromising rejoinder!

The next day, bright and early, two of us put up the stall. It was situated
between a man arranging massive piles of vegetables and a stall covered
with an extraordinary collection of bric-a-brac, china and old clothes.

I was initiated that morning into one of the most important
requirements of a Ministry of Food display. This was a very large platter of
a colourful, and beautifully arranged, vegetable salad, made from grated
raw beetroot, carrots, turnips, swedes, cabbage and whatever other
vegetables were in season at the time.

It was important that everyone ate plenty of vegetables, especially raw
vegetables, because these provided essential vitamin C. Oranges, lemons
and grapefruit and other citrus fruit were unavailable. It was difficult to
persuade people that raw vegetables were palatable as well as healthy. Up
to the beginning of the Second World War we had not been a nation of
salad, or vegetable eaters. Vegetarians were simply regarded as cranks.
Vegetables were badly cooked too – boiled to a mush in vast quantities of
water. The tradition, passed down from mother to daughter, was to use a
good pinch of bicarbonate of soda in the vegetable water to maintain
some colour. Salad was regarded as 'rabbit food' by most people,
especially men. But now, with depleted quantities of meat and fish and
virtually no poultry to be found, we all had to look at vegetables as a
source of nutritious food. In my opinion it was during the war that the
British learned to cook vegetables well.

As well as freshly prepared salad, the display included several cooked
dishes and one or two cakes. There were jars of bottled fruits too. It was
early spring at the time and there would soon be summer fruits and
British tomatoes (none were imported during those wartime days) to
preserve for leaner months. These store cupboard foods helped make
meals more interesting.

My acting experience had taught me how to project my voice, but it was
my market stall days that gave me a chance to develop a real fairground
approach to demonstrating. With one fellow stallholder on my left
bellowing out the price of his cauliflowers (3d, not much more than 1p)
and another on my right trying to foist the contents of her attic on an
unsuspecting public, it was a job to attract an audience. I lured the public

Weekly wartime rations

Butter – 2 oz/50 g

Cheese – 2 oz/50 g. There were times when this rose to 4 oz/100 g or even 8 oz/225 g (vegetarians had more and surrendered their meat coupons).

Eggs – one a week, sometimes only every two weeks, so the packets of 12 dried eggs a month were very welcome. This is why eggless cake recipes were useful – they are still popular today for those allergic to eggs.

Margarine and cooking fat – 4 oz/100 g each. There were periods when this was cut slightly.

Meat – 2 oz/50 g

Milk – from 2 to 3 pints/1.2 to 1.5 litres, according to availability. This was supplemented by 1 packet of dried milk monthly.

Sugar – 8 oz/225 g. If that sounds generous, remember we could buy only 1 lb/450 g preserves each month, so the sugar had to be kept to make jam when fruit was available, as well as being used for all other cooking purposes. There were times when we could buy extra sugar for preserving.

Sweets – 12 oz/350 g per month.

Tea – 2 oz/50 g a week.

Vegetables and fruits were mostly unrationed (but were fairly limited except in summer).

Fish was unrationed but was scarce, of a limited variety and not very fresh.

Bread and oatmeal were unrationed. These were eaten in quantity.

Expectant mothers, babies and young children had extra milk and bottled orange juice.

The points system

The monthly points system, which ran in conjunction with rationing, allowed each person a certain amount of choice. Each person was allowed 16 points per month which would allow you to buy, say, a can of fish or meat, or 2 lb/900 g dried fruit or 8 lb/3.6 kg of split peas.

to my stall by holding up an appetising cake or a pie and shouting out how the children would love it. Once I'd gathered a small crowd I could do my real job of getting over important nutritional advice.

By the time rationing had been in force for a while, everyone became much more willing to try new ideas. Meat dishes were the problem, and corned beef, sometimes forming part of the meat ration, and at other periods obtainable on the points system, was used to make **Corned Beef Hash**, **Fritters** and many other dishes.

During the last few years, there has been a deal great deal of interest in the diet of the Second World War; some nutritionists believe that people were fitter then than we are today and that the diet was healthier than most modern diets. Is that really true?

Take a look at the weekly rations on the previous page. They do accord with some modern ideas – plenty of vegetables, flour and oats, only a little meat and dairy produce. The food was nourishing all right, but it was also undoubtedly *boring*. Nutritionists forget one important point about the war: the spirit of the people. It was this wish to 'pull together' with the men doing the fighting and the families suffering air raids, that encouraged us to put up with this diet. Our duty was to keep healthy. Women were proud to be known as 'The Kitchen Front'.

While I was in East Anglia I ran several sessions at the Fruit Preservation Centres, held in various village and school halls. Groups of women would gather together to make preserves from locally grown fruit and specially supplied sugar. The recipes were formulated by the Ministry of Food, to make sure the preserves would be suitable for storage and then for sale to the public, as part of the monthly preserve ration.

The sessions were not entirely happy ones, for most women were very experienced in making preserves according to their own recipes. They were disinclined to be told what to do. 'Young woman I was making jam before you were born – and this is how I do it.' How many times I heard that announcement! I sympathised – no doubt they *were* wiser than I was, but my brief was to make sure they followed the recipes exactly. I still find myself inspecting jars of jam, or other preserves, to check on the sugar content, as this plays an important part in ensuring jam keeps. At the back you'll find my favourite recipe for **Black Cherry Jam**, together with general hints on jam-making.

During the war we became, to a large extent, one large community, sharing common worries. Money and class mattered far less than they had in the past. Even so, in these country communities it was one or two middle and upper class women who protested about being given instructions. Humbler jam-makers would never disagree with someone they felt to be 'above' them, though I did see them exchanging sly smiles when I insisted that *everyone* followed the prescribed recipe.

I helped the scientific division of the Ministry in assessing the vitamin content of cooked vegetables in school canteens. I had to smile at the various elaborate methods used to check the vitamin C content of cabbage – when any cook worthy of the name could see there was none left in the greyish mass lying sodden in the bottom of the pan. School dinners were one important innovation of that period, to help mothers who were working, and to ensure our children were adequately fed.

I had been back to Lincoln once while Bob was still there. As usual, trains were delayed and the journey from Cambridge seemed endless. While it was lovely to be with Bob, I came away absolutely shattered. The young men I knew had all aged so terribly. The crews were working desperately hard, for in 1942 there were huge losses and not enough trained personnel to replace them. It was the same men flying out on raids time after time.

In June, 1942, Bob became a Gunnery Leader. This meant he was in charge of all gunners in his Squadron; just after this he was promoted to the rank of Flight Lieutenant.

We managed to spend some time together in London, where I met Bob's mother and sister and enjoyed getting to know them. Bob's father had died when he was in his teens. Wartime romances were very unlike those of peacetime: we never knew how long one could have together, so engagements and the usual getting together of families had to be delayed.

In the late autumn of 1942 I left the Ministry of Food for a very happy reason: I was expecting a baby. I said I would consider returning at a future date, but made no commitment.

Like many pregnant young wives of that period, I went home to mother. Bob was being transferred to various RAF stations and, except in the case of commanding officers, wives were neither welcome nor allowed on operational stations. I must confess I was glad to stop working, because I had been unwell. I was suffering from a grumbling appendix, and what with that and the usual ailments of early pregnancy I found I was horribly sick, day after day. Winifred Hargreaves was wonderful, giving me less vigorous jobs and encouraging me to eat well and 'drink up your milk'. Doctors were very overworked, because so many members of the medical profession were on active service. Those that were left had little time to deal with such normal matters as pregnancy I consulted a woman doctor in Cambridge about the unending sickness. 'Take more sugar in your tea and go for plenty of brisk walks,' was her not very helpful advice.

Just before Judith was born my brother arrived home. There was much family rejoicing. The last time I had seen Philip was in 1940 after I had moved to Lincoln. He was in Hull, having guns fitted to his ship which up to that time had been unarmed. He was the officer in charge of supervising this work. I saw my young brother in a new light – brisk, efficient and very much in command.

In 1941 his ship had been bombed by the Germans at Crete. When they met and compared notes later, Bob and Philip decided they must have been in that area at the same time – Bob fighting in the air and Philip bringing 700 tons of essential ammunition for our troops fighting in Greece. Philip's ship did not sink, so the crew were able to get their belongings off it. It was hit again and caught fire. On his way home on another ship sailing via Durban, South Africa, Philip was asked by the shipping company to serve on a ship plying between South Africa and India. This ship had run into some problems with a Japanese submarine, and he was home to report to the Admiralty – and to marry the girl he had left behind. He brought with him a container of canned foods purchased abroad to help his wedding celebrations go with a swing.

Of course it wasn't only those on active service who suffered during the war. The calm acceptance of extraordinary events and constant danger was shown by civilians too. Friends of mine living in London survived raids on *two* houses, both of which were destroyed by bombs, by hiding under an elderly dining table.They spoke about the incidents as if describing a rather tedious shopping trip. So much has been written about air raids that there is no need for me to add much. We were fortunate in Barnet, for we were on the outskirts of London and so suffered little real damage, although we had plenty of disturbed nights. It is funny the silly things I do remember. When the London and Hertfordshire warnings both sounded we retired to the shelter, where we had bunks, and we made ourselves as comfortable as possible. For several weeks we shared this place with a very large spider. I have never been frightened of spiders since then: he, or she, was such a lovely normal thing in the middle of all the noise and fear.

Judith was several months old when my mother persuaded me to consider returning to work. I was very happy living with her, and adored looking after the baby, but there was not a great deal to do and I had too much leisure time – much of which was spent worrying about my husband's safety. The news of flying casualties was very grim. I enquired from official sources about the hope of finding a reliable person to look after Judith and it sounded quite out of the question. I went to the Ministry of Food and reported that there was no possibility of my returning in these circumstances. Mother was still teaching and so I couldn't leave her to look after the baby.

Imagine my amazement when I returned from shopping one day, soon after this interview, to find a trained nannie, sent by the Ministry of Labour, waiting to meet me. Dorothy Sargent was 28 and single. She was exempted from essential war work because she had an elderly mother at home and because she suffered from asthma. Working in a factory was out of the question. Back to my familiar work I returned, but this time in the London area. I enjoyed this very much for it was such a busy time, but some of my work was in the evenings and I was worried about the ever-increasing night-time raids.

Then I had a stroke of luck. The Ministry of Food had been running Advice Bureaux in both Harrods and Selfridges but were going to close them because thy felt their staff were needed elsewhere. Harrods protested – they felt their customers needed the help – so it was agreed that if Harrods would employ a Ministry-approved person to organise it, support would be given from the Ministry's headquarters and it could continue in that store. Harrods asked me to run the bureau, and although Headquarters were not delighted since I was also needed for my other work, they had to agree since anyone who was married and had a child could not be made to work in a specific place. This job was ideal. I would be home just as Dorothy was leaving and my mother wouldn't have to look after Judith in the evenings.

I owe a great deal to my years at Harrods, running the bureau there. I gave cookery demonstrations every morning and afternoon and on Saturday mornings. Eleven demonstrations each week means thinking up a great many new dishes as they couldn't be repeated too often. I made use of the official material issued by the Ministry, of course, but these recipes were not sufficient for my needs – I had to create my own dishes from the restricted demonstration rations available.

There is a lot of hard grind in this aspect of the work, even if you enjoy it, as I did and still do. You have to consider the time of year, the needs of the moment and the foods available, and then you start experimenting. Many ideas come from travelling, or eating in other people's homes and restaurants. You taste a dish, analyse it mentally. Yes, it's good, but wouldn't it be better if you changed the herbs or spices, or perhaps added more vegetables? All these factors help create a new recipe.

My audiences at the demonstrations were a great help in my search for new ideas. Although the majority of people who attended each session were new faces, there were some regulars I got to know well. I learned a lot about their needs as far as food was concerned.

I was sometimes asked to plan the menu for a special event. Invariably my first question had to be: 'What food have you got?' and we started from there. Planning a dinner party menu when you are told the only available food was a can of sardines, plus the week's meat ration for one person, certainly strained my creative ability!

My audiences contributed many ideas and would pass on the results of their own experiments and tell me family recipes. These were extremely interesting, for many came from other countries. London – and Harrods – was full of refugees seeking shelter in Britain. It was not possible to make many of these dishes for the ingredients were unavailable in wartime. I had to wait for the the years ahead. Typical of these were authentic **Strudels**, **Goulasch**, **Sachertorte**, **Escalopes** of various kinds, **Hazelnut Roulade** and **Linzertorte**.

Some of the dishes, such as **Liver Dumplings**, **Dolmas**, **Macaroni Soufflé** (dried eggs made edible, but not excellent, soufflés), were extremely practical and I enjoyed passing on the recipes to my audiences.

The Ministry of Food ensured their home economists were given as much help as possible. They arranged courses on the preservation of foods as well as on nutrition and special cookery demonstrations. One of them was given by Czech cooks and their recipes for **Fruit Dumplings**, yeast cakes and their very interesting **Potato Soup** became firm favourites.

Wartime recipes often include the words, 'a tomato and onion, if available'. Virtually no out-of-season foods were imported, so you were wise to bottle tomatoes and store, or dry, onions grown in summer. We all became experts in bottling and pickling. Fruit bottling became an art. Some women's organisations held displays of their artistic, as well as practical, skills. Every piece of rhubarb would be exactly the same length and arranged like a jigsaw so the pieces fitted into the jar in a perfect pattern. Jars of apples had a blackberry in the centre of each ring.

British gardens offered a strange sight in those days. 'Dig for Victory' was an important slogan. Flower beds were replaced by rows of potatoes, carrots and other vegetables, or in smaller gardens these essentials could be seen nestling among cherished rose bushes.

No restaurant of the time, however smart, was allowed to charge more than 5s (25p) for a meal, so chefs in leading hotels had to exercise their imagination to produce appealing menus within that price range.The food served was nutritious and helped people to eke out their rations at home by eating out occasionally. Factory canteens served cheap food too. Bakers were not allowed to ice cakes, even for a wedding. They would cover a very plain and uninspiring fruit cake with a round of white cardboard to make it look good! There was no rule about how you used your sugar ration so, when there was a wedding in the family, friends and relatives of the bride would contribute small amounts of icing sugar so she could have a proper cake. I kept my icing skills up to scratch because I was often asked to ice wedding cakes.

When the war news was very bad – or if the public were feeling unhappy about a further cut in rations – I made my demonstrations as light-hearted as possible. On several occasions I was told by the management, 'Make them laugh, Marguerite'. I made the audience practise tossing **Pancakes** or some such childish antic. It was easier to toss pancakes when they were made with the rather heavy wartime flour!

Many of the women, and a few of the men, who came to my demonstrations at Harrods had to learn how to cook, as well as deal with rationing. They had had staff to cook for them but, as the war went on, they lost most of their employees, who went to work in factories or joined the forces. Many of these people were elderly, so it was hard for them to adjust to dealing with all their household chores, including cooking. As the months and years went on, I could tell from their conversation that they were settling down well to these tasks – particularly the cooking.

Years later, when I was shopping in Harrods, I met one of these women. She greeted me, 'My dear, I am so grateful for all you taught me, I now have a cook, but I never allow her to be wasteful. I keep all the treacle, syrup and honey in the wardrobe. When cook wants any she comes to me and I measure it out for her.' To appreciate this strange conversation you need to have seen this lady. Even during the war years and, in spite of clothes rationing, she was exquisitely dressed. The thought of her diving into the wardrobe to measure out black treacle made it difficult to keep a straight face. I can't remember suggesting that food should be kept in the wardrobe, but I did emphasise the importance of not wasting food. You could be prosecuted for deliberately throwing away edible ingredients.

At last on 8 May, 1945 came VE (Victory in Europe) day. Although those who had members of their family in the Far East had to wait until 15 August for VJ (Victory in Japan) day before celebrating, it meant an end to the feared bombs, doodle-bugs and rockets which had haunted the night hours. We could go to bed without listening for the sirens, and listen to the radio or read the paper without hearing or seeing accounts of loss of life. My sister, now qualified as a primary school teacher and teaching in Edgware, was living at home with us at this time. We settled down to enjoy a quiet evening. Our mother objected, 'You girls (it is fascinating how one is always a 'girl' to one's mother, I was nearly 30 at the time, and my sister was 22) should go to London and join in the celebrations'. So we did. Never will we forget being part of the huge crowd in front of Buckingham Palace, singing, cheering and even shedding tears at the sight of the Royal Family and Winston Churchill. Foreigners accustomed to the reticent and restrained British would have been amazed. Complete strangers danced together and hugged each other. These carefree celebrations were a manifestation of the spirit of comradeship that prevailed during the War. We had all been in it together, and we had won through.

CHAPTER 5

On the Box!

I doubt if anyone was sufficiently optimistic to expect food rationing to end immediately after hostilities ended; but we would have been horrified if we had known that it would last until 1954. The reasons for this are fairly obvious – our ships had to bring back troops and materials from the various theatres of war around the world and we learned that much of the population of Europe was starving and their needs had to be met. Clothes and soap rationing also continued for some time. But we could now buy nylon parachute material without clothing coupons and we all began to make more glamorous undies.

As we entered the 1950s the number of foods that were unrationed increased. The fact that we could buy a little poultry, fish and a greater variety of fruits made catering easier and more interesting. To have citrus fruits again pleased me more than anything. And fresh bananas became available again. Children tasting their first bananas reacted differently. Some found the texture and flavour so unfamiliar that they wondered what all the fuss had been about! Just before the advent of fresh bananas, we had supplies of the dried variety and they were very popular in **Baked Bananas** (the recipe gives alternative ideas for using the fresh fruit).

In 1945, when the war ended, none of the familiar restrictions on food seemed to matter: we were so thankful to be at peace. But, inevitably after the first period of joy passed, we did grumble and fret about our limited food resources. Several foods new to the British made their appearance during this time. Supplies of salt cod (bacalao) came to augment the stocks of fresh fish – so many of our fishermen had been in the Merchant or Royal Navy and our fishing fleets were badly depleted. This fish, which had to be soaked for 24 hours before use, is a great favourite in the rest of Europe, and there were plenty of good recipes. It was not, however, to the taste of British families. Even less popular was canned snoek, a fish not unlike tuna in texture, that came from South Africa.

My most vivid memories are of experimenting with whalemeat. Even as I write I can remember that unique smell – a combination of meat, fish and strong oil. I was thankful that the whalemeat period was brief, for while the cooked dishes were edible, I loathed preparing the flesh. Nowadays the idea of eating this wonderful creature is utterly repellent.

During 1944 and 1945 I had been asked to give several radio broadcasts by the BBC, as part of their early morning daily *Kitchen Front* series. I repeated some of the ideas I had found most popular in my demonstrations. A wide range of people took part in these broadcasts, actors, comediennes, medical experts – anyone who had something to contribute in the realm of cookery, food and nutrition. Undoubtedly the most popular contributor was the Radio Doctor, Charles Hill (later to become Lord Hill). He gave his regular advice in a wonderfully fruity voice that educated, and cheered, his listeners.

On 7 October, 1946, a new afternoon programme came on the air – one that is still very much loved. It was *Woman's Hour*. I can't claim to have been one of the guests on the first day, but I *was* a speaker on the second. At that time the programme was introduced by a man – Alan Ivamey. On this first *Woman's Hour* broadcast I was asked to spend extra time answering 'phoned-in questions. I agreed of course and then discovered that my questioners were all in the Navy. Their questions surprised me: how to make a perfect **Egg Custard**, how to get a good textured sponge, ideas for new puddings. These were not the kind of things I had expected to preoccupy our gallant and stalwart Navy!

I participated in many *Woman's Hour* cookery broadcasts in the following years. Gradually their format changed as the producers found it better to provide new ideas and advice on a wide range of cookery subjects rather than simply give one or more recipes. Radio is not the ideal medium for detailed recipes as listing ingredients one by one takes a long time. As I broadcast mine, someone would sit across the table writing them down as I spoke and I watched their pen, so I could adjust my speed of delivery. Even so, I would get a few letters that said, 'Madam,' (people always address you as Madam when they are not pleased with you) 'Do you think we are shorthand writers that you give the ingredients so quickly?' and an equal number of letters that complained, 'Do you think we are slow-witted that you give the recipes so slowly?' Giving ideas and suggestions on the other hand meant that you could paint a picture for people to visualise. They had no need to write down details.

I have met many interesting people on that programme, two of whom I must mention. I owe a debt of gratitude to that wonderful actress, Dame Sybil Thorndyke. During her interview she was asked if she ever felt nervous before she walked on the stage, to which she replied, 'Very frequently and I find that what helps me is to take a number of long, slow, deep breaths just before I make my entrance.' Thank you, Dame Sybil. How valuable I found that advice in the years ahead, when I faced vast audiences at the London Palladium and elsewhere. The other person I shall never forget is Dame Margot Fonteyn. She was charming on the programme but, my real memory is of following her down the street, as she left Broadcasting House just ahead of me. We lesser mortals walked along the pavement – that slight, beautifully erect, figure seemed to float.

In November, 1947, came one of the most exciting events of my career. I was invited to be responsible for the cookery part of the new one-hour television magazine programme being started by the BBC called *Designed for Women*. Up to that time I had seen just two television programmes. Neither had anything to do with cookery, so I knew absolutely nothing about this medium. I was asked to come to the studio at Alexander Palace with all the food and equipment I needed for a dish that required just one boiling plate (there was some doubt as to whether more ambitious cooking facilities would be available) and, as the live programme was on the air round about teatime, to choose something suitable for that meal.

I decided to make easy doughnuts – made without yeast and with dried egg. Because of the shortage of fat these were shallow-fried and rather flat, not unlike fritters.

I am happy to report that my eight-minute doughnuts became very popular. They are rather different from today's doughnuts but are quick and easy to make. Simply blend 225 g/8 oz self-raising flour, 25 g/1 oz sugar, 1 egg and 4 tablespoons milk. Drop spoonfuls of the thick batter into a little hot fat or oil. Fry steadily on both sides until firm and golden in colour. Drain and toss in sugar. They made a good television recipe, as the viewer could watch them rising and browning in the pan. After that programme I was asked to become the regular cook in these afternoon programmes, which at first took place monthly – the hours of television in those days were relatively short. For the December 1947 Christmas programme that much admired television chef, Philip Harben, and I joined forces with our suggestions for a meal – still spartan I am afraid.

I look back on those early days of television with great pleasure – they were such fun and we felt like pioneers. Since there were so few studios at Alexandra Palace I met many people who were not concerned with our programme, but waiting to rehearse a musical event, a play, a discussion or a dance. Quite often they would be tucked in an odd corner of the studio while we were getting ready and there was a great feeling of camaraderie between everyone working at Ally Pally in those early days.

Early in January, 1948, I returned home from participating in the month's TV programme to a very unexpected, and tragic, event. My mother had died suddenly from a coronary. She had not appeared ill in any way and was still teaching and looking forward to taking a group of children from her class to see a special musical show in London just before the end of the Christmas school holidays.

As she was only 58, it was a bitter blow. I know I speak for my brother and sister as well as myself, when I say that she was not only a wonderful parent but a true friend to each of us, always encouraging, always ready to listen and advise, but never trying to force her opinions on us. The fact we have all had such happy and rewarding careers is very much due to her help and encouragement.

I would like to reproduce part of a letter the Headmaster of her school sent us. In it he says:–

> Your Mother was more than a member of the staff.
> Believe me, she was a radiance. She radiated
> kindness, tolerance, good-will, tact and humour.
> She mothered us, cheered us, gently reproved us,
> and always made us into the happiest family a
> school staff room has ever known.

Perhaps this explains why, during the war, young servicemen and women who had once been my mother's pupils called upon her to tell her of their progress. When I gave demonstrations in the theatres of large halls throughout the country, many people came to my demonstrations, not really to see me, but to tell me they had been taught by my mother and how she had helped them throughout their school careers.

Judith, only four, was so grieved at the death of her grandmother that she was ill for several weeks. Harrods, where I was still working, were wonderful and allowed me plenty of time to stay at home with her.

From around the end of 1948 our attitude to food began to change. Although still short of many ingredients, we knew better times lay ahead and everyone was full of excitement at the thought of creating more interesting meals. I think I would say that there were three distinct groups that needed help. First, there were the young women who had had little chance to learn anything about the art of cooking. They needed advice on basic cookery skills, both on television and in my demonstrations. Secondly there were many older women who remembered the dishes they used to enjoy, prior to 1939. They wanted recipes to help them cook the good old pre-war traditional British fare. The third group were anxious to learn about new dishes. Some had heard of interesting ways of cooking food from their husbands, sons or daughters who had been in the services in various parts of the world. It is said that the pleasures of scampi were brought to our attention by servicemen returning from Italy. I give at the back two of the simplest, but most interesting, ways of serving them – **Scampi Spumante** and **Scampi Capriccio**.

Bob had now been demobbed from the RAF. At the end of his period of flying in 1944, by which time he was a squadron leader, he was given an extremely interesting posting. He went to West Africa as the relieving commanding officer of the various RAF staging posts, so had the chance to see such fascinating places as Kano, Accra, Maiduguri. It was while in that part of Africa that he enjoyed their very hot curries; **Chicken Chop** (West African Chicken Curry) is one of his favourite dishes. During this period he had the exalted rank of Acting Wing Commander.

In 1947 Bob resumed his job as a buyer for Waltons, a large fruit chain and, as his work was largely in the South of England he lived with his mother in Hove during the week, only coming up to Barnet at weekends.

The summer after my mother's death, my sister decided to go and live in Norway. She was engaged to a Norwegian, Egil Moen, who was training to be a lawyer. She felt it was better to establish herself as a teacher of English in Oslo and save towards their future home, rather than continue to teach in England and go to Norway just at holiday time.

At Harrods we opened a second bureau to give demonstrations of all the latest appliances that seemed to arrive daily on the market. I had assistant home economists, so running the two bureaux was not difficult. We enjoyed demonstrating the first modern compact pressure cookers which were valuable for saving cooking time and also saving fuel – there was still a national shortage of fuel. In addition to the demonstrations in the bureaux, I was invited to give a showing to the press of this revolutionary way of cooking. The early pressure cookers were not quite as safely constructed as they are today. It was possible to open the lid with some pressure still left inside the pressure pan. Just before she left to work in Norway, my sister used a new pressure cooker to cook the meal. I arrived in the kitchen just in time to see the leaf spinach ascending to the kitchen ceiling! The pressure had dropped in the cooker, but there was still enough to cause this minor explosion. The safety devices on the cookers of today make such an accident virtually impossible.

The first electric mixers and labour-saving liquidizers (blenders) were making their appearance. Everyone suddenly became far more interested in trying their hand at making soups, such as home-made **Cream of Chicken** and **Iced Fruit Soup**, as they could dispense with sieves.

We demonstrated the latest cookers, the newest refrigerators and even the latest home laundry equipment, while still giving our regular cookery demonstrations in Harrods Food Hall.

Between 1947 and 1950 I wrote three cookery books for Harrods: *Recipes by Harrods*, *Harrods Second Cookery Book* and *Pressure Cooking by Harrods*. The dishes selected for my demonstrations on television and in the latest Harrods book show how many more interesting foods were coming on to the market.

There was a plague of pigeons during this time and these were harming valuable crops, so I was asked by the Ministry of Agriculture to show interesting dishes using these birds on television. Two I demonstrated were **Pigeon Cutlets** and **Pigeon and Mushroom Ragôut**. Dishes using game were popular, and **Salmis of Grouse**, which is equally good with pheasant, partridge, or even duck, was a great favourite. Good fish was beginning to appear once more and I was able to show a wider variety of fish dishes, ranging from the economical **Devilled Herrings** to the more luxurious **Sole Normandy**. Even in 1950 we were still short of eggs and although we had become very experienced in using dried eggs, I think most of us longed for the old-fashioned kind. Cream was still hard to get hold of and even in *Harrods Second Cookery Book*, written in 1950, I concentrated on ways of making mock cream. Cheese was much more plentiful and so cheese dishes, such as vegetarian **Cheese Cutlets** were much in demand. There was still only a very limited variety of cheeses – good old 'mousetrap' would just about sum it up!

Bob and I had a holiday in the New Forest. We were disgusted by the quality of food on offer, which was pretty ghastly, even for that era. This led to my making a remark that was to direct the next change in my life. I said: 'If I couldn't do better than that I'd eat my hat.' We thought of my moving to the south coast, where Bob needed to be for his job with Waltons, and opening a guest house. The more we talked about the idea, the more we liked it. It would mean that I would be at home so much more. We went house-hunting. Fortunately, as future events turned out, we found a house in Hove, Sussex, that would be the right size for a small guest house or a family home. We went ahead with the purchase.When I told Harrods, they asked if I would continue to come in two days a week. I agreed because I had hated the idea of leaving altogether.

So in March 1951 we moved into 'Hovecrest'. Bob had managed to get essential work done – not easy because at that time the amount of money we were allowed to spend on decorations and home improvements was severely restricted by the Government.

I engaged a housekeeper and a good daily help and we found a splendid local school for Judith. I seemed to spend all my waking hours sewing table mats, making curtains and shopping for extra bed-linen, furnishings, china and glassware – still difficult to obtain. We gave ourselves a few months of private life together and then in the summer of 1951 we were ready to welcome our first guests. I was still doing radio and television and travelling to London twice weekly.

Our first season was a busy one: we were completely booked, with waiting lists of people wanting to visit us. I was of course able to get excellent food from Harrods, as well as locally. Everything was home-made, as our visitors expected. I managed to get hold of two very special attractions which proved popular with our guests: capercailzie (a wild cock, the size of a turkey) and the most wonderful Polish geese. They had breasts so plump that you could carve really good slices. Sadly, neither are available in the shops today – at least I have never found them.

We closed for the winter and opened up again the following Easter. Just before we were due to open I had a busy time at Harrods, and a TV programme to do. The day before our first guests were due, I travelled to London and left my housekeeper to do the flowers. I had ordered early asparagus as one of the ingredients for the next day's lunch.

I arrived home rather tired, expecting to find an orderly kitchen, with flowers suitably arranged around the guest house. Instead I discovered chaos. It turned out that our housekeeper was a little too fond of the gin. She had been by herself all day and had indulged not wisely, but too well. The kitchen floor was strewn with flowers, among which I could discern the asparagus – it looked a little like the Nice carnival of flowers. Tired as I was I had to buckle down, sort out this little muddle and get ready for

Easter. We were completely booked up for the rest of the season. At Whitsun that year all of us had 'flu, not badly but sufficient to make us realise that running a catering business, however small, was no mean task. Bob quietly shut himself away and wrote polite letters to everyone who had expected to come and stay with us during the next months. Regrettably, he said, we had decided to close the guest house.

Was the guest house a success? Yes and no. Yes, because so many people wanted to stay with us, and we met many interesting people, even if some were a trifle eccentric. There was the woman with a passion for collecting wild flowers: each day she would disappear and come back laden with armfuls. She used all my spare vases and tumblers for flower arranging, and I am not at all convinced that she had the well-being of the countryside at heart.

Then we had a charming old lady, whose daughter turned out to be a drug addict. She turned up at the guest house and started to torment her delightful mother and we found ourselves in the middle of an unpleasant domestic drama involving the police.

But it was a failure because I overlooked one very important point. If you run any sort of catering business you do so to *make* not *lose* money. Bob described our guest house as being the best philanthropic institute on the south coast, and he was not far wrong. Still you live and learn, and the guest house did give me the opportunity to please a number of people with some of my favourite dishes, such as **Asparagus Cheese, Globe Artichokes with Fish Paté, Vichysoisse, Crown Roast of Lamb, Roast Duck with Prune and Apple Stuffing, Syllabubs** and Wine Creams.

Harrods asked me to return full-time, which I felt unable to do, so both bureaux were closed. I still have a great fondness for this wonderful store and enjoy my visits there today, walking through the food halls and recalling those busy, delightful days during and after the War.

CHAPTER 6

Infinite Variety

After I left Harrods I imagined life would be quieter. I did not expect to be idle, for I hoped I would continue my TV and radio broadcasts and also do more writing. Late in 1948 I became the regular cookery writer for the London *Evening News* – I was so sorry my mother had not lived to see me writing for this newspaper. I thoroughly enjoyed because I had to keep completely up-to-date with events on the food front. It was quite normal for the features editor of the paper to ring me and say he had learned there would be a glut or shortage of some particular food, and could he have an article on the subject by the next morning. This meant my hastily writing recipes for cooking the foods available at that moment, or giving helpful advice if some basic food became scarce due to bad weather, or other unexpected events. This was quite different from planning cookery articles for magazines, where I was writing for issues to be published weeks or months ahead.

During this period I was asked to write four cookery books. The first three were all published by Phoenix House and were called *Cakes and Baking, Invalid Cookery* and *Learning to Cook,* which was especially for children and young people who because of food shortages had never had a chance to cook before . Later in the 1950s I was commissioned to write *Cooking for Bachelors and Bachelor Girls* by the publishers, Robert Hale. These were an interesting selection of subjects, and I think it right to say that they reflected the particular needs of that period. Many people were longing to get back to baking for their family, as in pre-war days, and my *Cakes and Baking* was based very much on classic and traditional recipes. As it was published in 1952 it does echo the fact that rationing, although not yet ended, was appreciably less restricted.

Invalid Cookery may sound a strange choice for a first selection of cookery books. But it was a very necessary title. During the war years there had been little time to worry about special diets but now suddenly there were requests for help. The book was written as a direct result of my series on television on this subject and the articles and booklet I wrote for the British Medical Association. For a time the BMA published a monthly magazine on sale to the general public. It covered a variety of subjects and my articles dealt with nutritious meals for everyone as well as special diets.

Young men and women, returning from the services, had had a taste of an independent life and now wanted to move away from the family home. Many were studying at universities and colleges and cooking for themselves, so *Cooking for Bachelors and Bachelor Girls* was produced to help them cook well with limited facilities and a restricted budget.

I found that I had a talent for writing cookery books, but how they have changed from the rather restrained publications that came on the market in the fifties. The book that brought me the most publicity was *Cookery in Colour*, first published in 1960 by a marvellous man – Paul Hamlyn, whose fame, and empire, have grown over the years. He is now chairman of the Octopus Group which includes many well known publishing companies.

When I first met Paul Hamlyn, his firm was quite small. I got to know everyone so well and many of the staff have stayed firm friends. I loved the feeling of being a part of the team in that enthusiastic organization and I am very grateful for all the assistance I was given. I have worked for other publishers too and have invariably found the work to be most pleasant. It is a great joy for a freelance in any field to have the opportunity to exchange ideas and learn from other people.

Cookery in Colour was an exceptional publication for the time. Nearly every one of the 1000 recipes was accompanied by a photograph, and the book was printed on tinted paper. It stood out in great contrast to the restrained cookery books that had been accepted as the norm up to then. So far *Cookery in Colour* has sold well over two million copies.

I can boast about the book since I was neither the designer nor the publisher. I think it made publishers realise just how much pictures helped their readers achieve professional-looking dishes. Nowadays we take beautifully produced and illustrated cookery books for granted.

The fifties was a wonderful period in which to do TV cookery as there was so much to show and so many subjects to cover. The most memorable programmes in 1952, and repeated in 1953, were those dealing with Christmas cookery. Turkeys were more plentiful by this time and so were many other seasonal ingredients. The Ministry of Food made sure there were plentiful supplies of dried fruit, fat, sugar and eggs in the shops so that we could cook a delicious **Christmas Cake** and **Christmas Pudding** of real pre-war quality. I felt quite strange when I broke four fresh eggs into a basin to make the Christmas cake – it had been so long since I had seen so many at one time! Wherever I have done demonstrations since, someone always pops up to tell me they still make those particular recipes. The BBC were inundated with requests for the recipes. Although they have been printed many times, I am including them in this book, for they emphasise that at long last Britain was returning to normal on the food front. At the back you will find the versions I made on TV at that time, plus hints on adding extra ingredients to make them richer.

Not every viewer was pleased with me – I used alcohol in both the cake and pudding and a number of people accused me of leading Britain astray. My favourite complaint dated from the 1953 programmes. I made the cake in one programme and on subsequent programmes showed how to coat this with marzipan and royal icing and suggested ways of decorating it. I was not a little surprised when the BBC told me they had received a complaint from a viewer who said, 'The cake was fine, but the icing was burnt to a cinder.'

I did a series on meat cookery, so people could learn to recognize various cuts of meat – remember that for years we had been used to buying 1s 2d (6p) worth of meat per week, which gave us no chance to be selective. I did similar programmes on fish, vegetable and fruit cookery. Oh! The joy of having a good selection of fish and being able to introduce ingredients such as red and green peppers, aubergines and various kinds of imported fruits. I tried to bring a little-known ingredient to the studio for each programme.

New foods were beginning to find a market. On one programme I made a quiche. I lost count of the number of times I was asked to repeat the word 'quiche' – few people had heard of it before.

We started a series on special cookery problems which were discussed on the programme. One of my guests had difficulty in balancing her housekeeping budget and I planned to cook several economical dishes and give her ideas to save money. During the run-through in the morning my guest had been very quiet: in fact it was difficult to get her to talk at all. During the programme in the afternoon, however, which of course went out live,she suddenly became a different character, verbally abusing her husband for his meanness and saying: 'You tell him, Marguerite, you just tell him he has to give me more money.' Not easy to deal with in front of the cameras!

The programme that attracted the most attention from the press was my bread-making show. When I got home after the programme, my husband had received a message that I was to contact the BBC at once – what on earth had gone wrong? It appeared there had been somewhat freak weather conditions that day and, during my bread-making, the BBC had received a telephone call from America to ask, 'Have you got a dame making a pud?' For a short time they had tuned in to our programme, so I was the very first British person to be received direct on American television.

Towards the end of the 1950s it was decided that cookery would take on a new look. The BBC Cookery Club was formed and I was made President. Each month I set the subject for a competition – it could be ideas for a special dinner party, a buffet, a family dish, based upon a certain food or dishes especially for children. I tested all the entries and picked the winner, who would be invited to come on the programme with me. This was interesting, for it showed just how many imaginative cooks there were in the country.

At the beginning of the sixties these particular magazine programmes ended. It was felt that after years of fairly domestic issues women were anxious to widen their horizons.

Whenever I appear on TV these days the producer often wants to include a clip of those early BBC programmes. Alas, not one of them was recorded.

Both the gas and electricity industries had been nationalized by this time and they had large teams of home economists who carried out cookery demonstrations for the public. From time to time, however, large-scale demonstrations were planned. For these major events 'media cooks' such as myself, Philip Harben or John and Fanny Craddock (known together as as 'Bon Viveur' – to start with some people didn't even realise they were two people) would be invited to do the cooking. It was fascinating to see how different audiences reacted to these demonstrations. In some parts of the country the public was quietly appreciative; while in others they would clap after every dish was completed. In the early fifties I varied my dishes according to where I was demonstrating. At that time the north of England, Scotland and Wales had less inclination to try some of the newer recipes and foods that were trickling over from the Continent. Moreover, their shops didn't stock the necessary ingredients for these dishes. Gradually, of course, this changed and in later years supermarkets all over the country were stocked with the same goods.

Should I become tired and vague with all the travelling involved in these demonstrations, I would at least always know when I was in Wales. Long before the demonstration began the audience started to hum in tune with the recorded music being played as they entered the hall. After a time the hum became soft singing and finally full-throated and beautiful harmonies.

It was before one of the Welsh demonstrations that I was told a man wanted to speak to me. He was a fisherman, turned chef, who wished to acquaint me with the fact that he was a complete expert in all forms of cooking; he had a seat in the front row and he would nod if he felt I was doing things in a proper manner. Throughout the two hours of the demonstration I found myself instinctively looking towards that seat and waiting for the nod. I dread to think what he, or I, would have done if he had disapproved of my work!

Some of my time was spent acting as a consultant to various firms and this led to a completely unexpected request to combine cookery demonstrations with top variety acts. Jim Grover, sales director of Frenlite, a flour-producing firm, felt that this approach would appeal to people who might not come to an afternoon or evening performance of cooking alone. I agreed to participate in these new events, to be entitled 'Melody Fare'. The programme was two hours altogether, of which I had one hour, divided into three periods. These shows were to take place in large or city halls and theatres that accommodated hundreds of people.

The show began with the band and dancers and then I had my first perfectly straightforward cookery spot. I was followed by the comedian and singer(s) on the bill, who then handed back to me for more cookery. My final spot was different. We decided it would be good to end my part of the programme in a light-hearted manner, so I taught the comedian on the show – who over a period of time included such well known names as Cyril Fletcher, Richard Murdoch, Bill Pertwee – how to ice a cake, or make a trifle, or perform some other task where we could be sure they would create plenty of chaos. Dickie Valentine, who was then at the height of his popularity, was a singer on some of these shows. Imagine how I felt coming on stage after him to do a serious demonstration with the crowd of female admirers still screaming their appreciation! That delightful pair, Pearl Carr and Teddy Johnson, were with these shows for a long period.

We then heard that we were going to put on 'Melody Fare' at the London Palladium for several afternoon performances. Pearl said to me, 'You wait, Marguerite, when you realise you are on stage at the Palladium, you will feel quite different'. I replied, with complete sincerity at the time, 'I doubt it, for it doesn't mean the same to me, as to you professional variety people.' How wrong I was! The revolving stage moved around, my name was announced, the curtains parted and I felt the great thrill and feeling of panic that must hit everyone who has the honour of appearing at this famous theatre. Later I took part in Palladium shows in which cooking was combined with fashion; I was asked to appear in a special dress at each entrance – no hardship for a woman. David Jacobs was the compère of these and my daughter was one of my assistants. She was just getting ready to start her career in public relations.

For these large-scale theatre presentations I had to choose the food I cooked very carefully. In a show that moved so swiftly, the dishes had to be quick to prepare and able to be left cooking, unattended, while the comedian, or singers, or band, were on stage. They performed with the cookers in the background and would not have appreciated performing while smoke billowed from the ovens! It was a joy at the Palladium to have my own part of the revolving stage. Although the stage was brilliantly lit the audience could see very little of the food being prepared at such long range, so I had to rely on my choice of words and the general effect to paint the picture. It was a little like doing a conjuring act: I learned to lift things high and to handle every ingredient and utensil with as much speed as possible. Such shows today would include large screens so that the audience could see everything clearly. I concentrated on imaginative ideas based on bacon and ham, for these cooked rapidly; luxurious dishes, in which eggs could be used with gay abandon, such as soufflés and meringue-topped desserts; attractively decorated cakes – all these were still a treat after years of shortages. Having whisked the egg whites for meringues or other desserts until they were stiff, I would turn the bowl upside down to prove the point – of course once I forgot to check whether the mixture was stiff. I can still hear the gasp of horror from myself and my audience when the frothy mixture fell out with a plop.

At the beginning of the programme I would always ask my audience to time the first dish, often a sponge to make a **Swiss Roll**, or a more

modern **Roulade**. They always made a complete mess of this simple task. If I asked them to tell me when eight minutes had elapsed I would start to hear calls of 'Time's up!' after three minutes. It didn't matter. I had made personal contact with my audience and that was essential. You see, I was learning how to be a variety artist.

I was on stage with Cyril Fletcher at Portsmouth and, in the final cookery spot, I was teaching him to make a trifle. It seemed that half the Navy were in the audience They had behaved with complete decorum during my more serious demonstrations, but now the fun had started they really let themselves go. I will leave you to imagine the comments! On my own I might have found the situation difficult, but Cyril's masterly knowledge of timing helped us turn their remarks to good account.

Even more unusual demonstrations were in store for me. Jim Grover, who organized 'Melody Fare', had another bright idea for filling a theatre for a week. To get a free ticket to the show, the public had to send, or hand in, packet tops from Frenlite flour (or other products in later years when this imaginative man moved to another firm). The evening's entertainment was to be completely filled by top-line variety artists – except for my spots. When I heard about this I was worried. 'Melody Fare' was basically a cookery show, plus variety. *This* was to be a variety show, plus cooking. The audience might well be unappreciative of straightforward cookery demonstrations interrupting their fun. My husband and I discussed this and felt that my part could be a horrible flop. We suggested that, instead of giving ordinary demonstrations, I should ask for male volunteers to come from the audience and cook. For the first shows they would make sponges. The idea was accepted by Frenlite. Cookers were to be provided and it was arranged that young home economists would be stationed by the cookers to assist volunteers.

The first of these weeks was at the famous Palace Theatre, Manchester. The artists rehearsed their routines all day. The bill was an impressive one: Geraldo and his Show Band provided the music, the dancers were drilled by Lionel Blair and the other artists were of the same calibre. The comedian Albert Modley was a great favourite in the north of England and he was on stage too. The moment came when I faced the audience and stepped forward to ask for my volunteers. Geraldo and Albert were poised at the side of the stage, ready to step in if I could not find volunteers or got into difficulties. Do you wonder that over the years I have become a great lover of variety? In fact in all the many shows of this kind we did, I never experienced any problems in getting men to come up on stage and cook. We had *too many* volunteers, possibly because some of the glamorous dancers guided them up on to the stage. While the men performed, I was able both to encourage them in their efforts, which were often quite hilarious, and also to talk about the merits of the flour and how to develop baking skills. Towards the end of the show my volunteers came up again to show the audience their freshly baked sponges. The look of triumph on their faces when they took the finished products out of the ovens was a pleasure to see. Oddly enough, no matter what extraordinary techniques the men had used to mix their sponges, they always turned out well. Perhaps correct technique is not as essential as we experts imagine.

These costly and elaborate demonstrations are a thing of the past but I still give a certain number of demonstrations each year: they give me such pleasure. They are a wonderful way of testing out recipes too. Not that I ever make a dish for the first time in front of an audience – all my recipes are tested in my kitchen first – but I watch the audience to see if they are interested in that particular type of cooking or enjoy using those ingredients. When there is an interval I talk to members of the audience – their questions and hints give me much food for thought. This love of demonstrating to an audience led to one of the most exciting periods in my cooking career – demonstrating across the other side of the world.

CHAPTER 7

My Travels Down Under

In 1961 we moved from Hove to Brighton, where we live to this day. We bought an orchard plot which was once part of the grounds of one of the large houses in Brighton and then discovered that Bob had a hidden talent. He designed the house and it was built exactly to his design. The garden was large enough to give me plenty of scope: I have inherited my mother's love of gardening.

It was from here, in 1964, that I embarked upon the longest, and certainly the most demanding, journey I have ever made. It was to Australia, where I had been engaged by the *Australian Woman's Weekly* to give cookery demonstrations on television and to live audiences in many major cities, starting in Sydney and ending up in Perth.

As I watched the English coastline disappear from the window of the Quantas plane, and there was nothing but sea to look at, I sat back to think about the time ahead. I was to spend nearly three weeks in America and Hawaii *en route* to Australia. Although this was chiefly a holiday period it would give me time to read, and re-read, my recipes and demonstration menus, so I would be as confident as possible when I arrived in Sydney.

This vacation would also enable me to catch up on some sleep. For the past few months I had been incredibly busy, with the minimum time for rest. There was my usual work of demonstrating and writing, and I had had to write extra articles for magazines to cover my time abroad. There were the dishes and menus to plan, type and send to Australia, after these had been tested with the flour, the other food products and wines that had been sent to me from Australia for the purpose. I don't think people appreciate just what subtle differences the choice of flour and fats make in baking cakes and various kinds of pastry. I was very pleased to have had the chance to test Australian products. Letters had been flowing backwards and forwards for months from Sydney, outlining the itinerary, telling me about the various firms who would be working with the *Australian Woman's Weekly* to sponsor my trip, and advising me what foods were scarce or plentiful in the country.

And now I was on my way. The journey didn't worry me, as I have always loved travelling, especially when it involves flying. But I was apprehensive at the thought of crossing the world to work in a country where I knew no one. How would the Australians accept an Englishwoman giving them advice about cookery?

My mind went back to the time, nearly a year before, when I had been summoned to Hamlyn's offices. I didn't know why until I arrived and met an impressive gentleman by the name of Tony, representing the *Australian Woman's Weekly*, who, at that time, was responsible for the distribution and sale of Hamlyn books in Australia. Paul Hamlyn was also present at the meeting, the purpose of which was to find out whether I was willing to work in Australia for some weeks and whether I was suitable for the job.

The questions came thick and fast about my experience in television and in giving cookery demonstrations and my availability the following year. It was a complete surprise to me and I was flattered, although I must confess I had never felt any particular desire to visit Australia.

When the questioning finally seemed to be at an end, Tony said, 'Ah yes, two more things they asked me to check,' and from a piece of paper he read, 'Are you la-di-da and are you an old bag?' I still remember the long silence and the look of horror on the faces of everyone else in the room. I laughed and said something like, 'So this is an example of the famous outspoken manner I can expect in Australia?' Tony wasn't at all abashed. It seemed quite logical to him to let me know just what he was told to find out.

I went home after this meeting, my mind buzzing with thoughts and doubts about the project. The proposed tour would be during late spring and summer, a period when I was less busy with demonstrations in Britain. Even so, it would entail a great deal of extra work beforehand to cover my absence. Another problem to consider was how much help I could expect from home economists in Australia. I had so much support in this country. All these things had to be considered. In the end Bob persuaded me to accept the offer. He stressed it was a unique opportunity for me and that he was confident I would enjoy working with Australians. He spoke from experience for he had been posted to the first Australian Bomber Squadron formed in Britain.

I left England on a morning early in May. It was a gloriously warm day. Everywhere looked beautiful and I hated leaving the garden: it was so full of colour. Although we all behaved as though this was a perfectly ordinary trip I felt very subdued on the journey to Heathrow – leaving Bob and Judith for so long was a big step. I was not to worry, they said, they could cope very well without me.

It was scorchingly hot when I arrived for my stopover in New York and I looked forward with great longing to a cool shower and a leisurely drink at my hotel. I had booked into one of the Hiltons. I found a pleasant and informative taxi driver, and I arranged that he would meet me on the following morning and take me around part of the city.

I walked up to the check-in desk at the hotel, waving the hotel's confirmation of my room reservation and accompanied by a hotel porter carrying my vast array of cases. I was told that the hotel had overbooked, sorry, the World Fair was on and the city was teeming with visitors. This was a bad start to my holiday. I made a fuss and the manager finally found me a very dingy room in a run-down hotel. I had little inclination to stay in much or eat in the hotel, but perhaps that was a good thing because I spent much of my time eating in small restaurants and sampling real American food.

During the sixties Britain started to discover some of the better known dishes of other countries, including those of America. Restaurant menus figured **Chicken Maryland**, that mixture of fried young chicken with fried bananas and sweetcorn fritters, and I was asked frequently for the recipe by readers and listeners. Modern nutritionists might well shake their heads at the amount of frying in that single dish, but it is very appetising, if properly prepared. People were interested in making **Cheesecakes** of various kinds and I was anxious to sample some of these to discover new flavourings. I found the portions of cheesecake served in restaurants so generous that they constituted almost a main dish. I loved the light iced mallows which were popular desserts; these are a form of ice cream based on marshmallows. (A recipe for **Pistachio Mallow** can be found at the back.) I sampled sherberts made with some of the exotic fruits which were just becoming known in Britain. We call sherberts by their more classic title – **Sorbets**. I tried their cakes, including **Angel Cake,** that light gateau which is a wonderful way of using up leftover egg whites. How I enjoyed some of the excellent **Salads**, several of which are true American classics.

My taxi driver showed me around New York. I was disappointed in Broadway. The first time I saw it was in the daytime and it seemed to be less colourful and exciting than I had imagined. So, eager to give it every opportunity to impress me, I returned at night to see if my opinion had changed. It hadn't; I still felt it to be a less than glamorous place. Central Park in May, on the other hand, was lovely and I enjoyed wandering through parts of that famous open space.

Two things I very much appreciated on this, my first time in America, were, first, the fact that iced water was automatically placed on your table as you sat down, whereas in Britain it was a long struggle to get water to drink with a meal, and, second, the friendliness of waiters and waitresses in restaurants. They looked as if they were pleased to see you and their farewell 'have a good day' was pleasant to hear. I know cynics say that this is just part of their training, and that it isn't genuine, but it did quite a lot for my morale at a time when it was pretty low. I was wondering why I said I would do this trip. Luckily, many better things were in store.

The first of these, when I boarded the Quantas plane again, was to find that I had the same cabin crew with whom I had flown the Atlantic. I had liked them very much and admired them too. The sixties was a period when a small number of people from Britain were emigrating to Australia to make a new life. Some had been on the plane on the first leg of my journey – and I couldn't help noticing the strained looks and tears on the faces of some of the women and children. They were taking a great step into the unknown – would it be the right one? The stewards and stewardesses seemed to know just the right things to say to them.

I poured out my tale of woe about the hotel in New York and they were duly indignant on my behalf. I also mentioned that I had one or two names of Australian airmen with whom my husband had flown, or caroused with, in Lincoln, and he had asked me to try and locate them in Australia. (I think he also wondered if any of them had become pilots with Quantas). I was ushered on to the flight deck to meet the captain and flying crew and ask them about these men. What an incredible experience! We were flying in perfect weather and the vista below was quite breathtaking. I shall always remember the dramatic scenery below us and the sun glinting on the peaks of the Rockies. None of the flying crew knew Bob's friends personally, but they had certainly heard of one: Micky Martin, a legendary hero, later to be knighted, and one of the outstanding Australian pilots of the war. (The crew were full of awe that my husband had known him.)

My next stop was San Francisco, where I was to stay for a few days. The sun was still shining as we circled over the city waiting to land and it was a wonderful chance to see the famous Golden Gate bridge. I felt some trepidation as I approached the hotel desk, but there were no problems with my room this time. I must record what happened the next morning when I ordered breakfast in my room. I asked for scrambled eggs, a surprising choice for me. I am sure most people would agree that for really **Perfect Scrambled Eggs** they must be cooked and eaten straight away, whereas in most hotels the dish seems to linger *en route* to the table, so they arrive in a half-cold, solid, unappetising mound.

Not so in this hotel! As the beautifully laid trolley was wheeled into my room the waitress was scrambling the eggs over a small spirit-stove – and they really were perfection.

It is strange what preconceived ideas we have about the food in other countries. I had been warned time and time again that I would not like American food: 'It all comes out of packets, you know.' What nonsense this turned out to be. Even during my brief stay in New York I had sampled many splendid fresh foods. In San Francisco I was to enjoy more.

When we are travelling in strange cities, my husband and I always like to find knowledgeable taxi drivers. I was singularly lucky to find a most helpful driver in San Francisco who recommended me to some fascinating places to eat down by the waterfront. There I sampled a truly memorable **Seafood Bisque** – a satisfying, creamy soup that is a meal in itself and a lovely sticky Creole-inspired **Crab Gumbo**. It used to be difficult to make in Britain because we lacked the essential ingredient, okra (ladies fingers), but now that vegetable is obtainable this is a dish well worth making.

I was introduced to the famous Cow Palace, where so many political events take place and somehow I got myself muddled up in a political rally at a hotel, where I had slipped in to have a cup of coffee. I was swept along by a crowd of women all wearing huge rosettes declaring their devotion to some politician or other, whose name I'm afraid I can't recall. It took time to extricate myself, find a quiet corner and have my coffee.

In San Francisco I also tasted a real American **Pecan Pie**, a dessert of great distinction, and one of the best known dishes served in the waterfront restaurants: **Cioppino**. I had imagined this to be an Italian dish but was assured that it had been created by the fishermen of San Francisco and that if I stayed long enough I would be able to sample many versions of the succulent and luxurious fish dish – each chef claiming his to the best. While I was there I learned that a true **Strawberry Shortcake** is made with a very light dough, and this is the recipe I have preferred ever since. I was glad to sample this since, as a strawberry addict, I knew I was missing the English season of this lovely fruit. The strawberries I tasted in America were delicious but perhaps missing the delicate sweetness of our berries.

On the day of my departure, my taxi driver friend took me to visit the Japanese Tea Gardens. I wandered around the beautiful surroundings and had a peaceful cup of tea. As we were leaving, I was introduced to Alf, another taxi driver. On hearing I was from England he said he had driven a gentleman from England around San Francisco who owned a ranch back home. I tried not to look too surprised at the thought of a ranch-owning Englishman and enquired who this might be. 'Duke Derby,' was the reply. 'When you get back to England and meet him would you say Alf sends his regards.' Alas I never met the the Earl of Derby or went to his 'ranch' so I never passed on the message.

My next port of call was Hawaii and this was where I did my homework. I have always told young student home economists that a good demonstration is rather like an iceberg – the audience sees just one-tenth of the work, but the hidden nine-tenths is of vital importance. This consists of planning the dishes, testing them, working out the order in which they will be cooked, so that everything is seen at its best at the end of the session. In addition you need to consider what to say as you make each dish. I always find that if for some reason I have not done this background work as well as I should, then, no matter how hard I try when I actually give the demonstration, I am disappointed and dissatisfied with it – and I am sure my audience shares that feeling.

I went through all my dishes one by one, planning the working order, and considering just what anecdotes and helpful information I could pass on while doing the cooking. Hawaii couldn't have been a better place to do this work. I had elected to have a chalet in the grounds of the hotel, so I would have plenty of peace for working. In fact, most of my studying was done on the beach. This really was like a picture postcard – golden sands, the bluest sky imaginable and blue sea with rolling surf. I had to be very strong- minded not to doze. From time to time it rained a little, but the rain was so gentle that it was hardly worth moving. When the sun came out I dried off almost immediately. In-between reading through recipes I could watch the very accomplished surfers ride the waves. It was certainly a joy to be in this paradise!

What about the food? In the hotel it was typically American. There were hamburgers with a wide variety of toppings, served at lunchtime on the beach. I have never been a lover of hamburgers but watching young and old tucking into them made me determined to find out if it was my method of making and cooking them that was wrong. I tasted hamburgers in several different places and must confess they still are one of my least favourite dishes, but I have included the recipe for the best **Hamburger** I know, along with the various tips given me by accomplished cooks of this popular dish.

Away from the hotel I discovered foods new to me. There were those delicious macadamia nuts, now available in Britain, and some varied dishes in which fresh coconut played an important part, such as **Shrimps in Lime and Coconut Sauce** and a **Coconut Cream Pie**. Although both these dishes are at their best made with fresh coconut, they are still delectable made with either desiccated or creamed coconut. Also, I tasted sweet potatoes and yams for the first time. Although similar in appearance and flavour, these vegetables come from different plants and yams are sweeter. The method of baking them with pineapple is a dish never to be forgotten. Now that both sweet potatoes and yams are plentiful in Britain I hope people will try the **Yam and Potato Bake**. And in our home no Christmas dinner is complete without roast sweet potatoes.

One of the minor problems associated with writing cookery books to be used in more than one country is the different names given to even everyday ingredients. I learned in Hawaii that in America the word 'prawn' is not used in recipes. Irrespective of their size, shrimps and prawns are all called 'shrimps'. In Britain, of course, shrimps are the very tiny shellfish, all too rarely seen in the fishmongers. The shrimps in their delicious lime and coconut sauce would have been called really plump prawns in Britain.

Like most visitors to Hawaii I attended an evening *luau*, a very special feast. Earlier in the day I had watched the preparations being made. A deep pit is dug and lined with leaves from banana trees – and I think I remember the organiser of the event saying that some tea leaves were added too – no, not from the pot, from the bush.

In this pit was placed a prepared pig and chickens. These were covered with more leaves, and cooked all day, ready for us to eat at night. It was a wonderful evening, stars shining, beautifully warm, and everyone in a truly relaxed mood ready to enjoy the mixture of pork and chicken served with local spinach. Was it delicious? Not really, it tasted rather odd, but it was enjoyable to sit and eat and watch graceful local dancers.

On my last day I chatted to some American holiday-makers. A woman sitting beside me asked, 'Where do you come from?' I felt that she might not know the town of Brighton so replied, 'In a seaside town, not far from London.' 'Is that in Europe?' she enquired. 'Yes,' I said. 'I have been to Europe,'she said. 'Did you go to London?' I asked. 'No, just Athens – but I expect it's all the same.'

I caught the eyes of several other American tourists who had heard this conversation. They shook their heads in disbelief. I must say this was the first time I had heard London dismissed quite so summarily!

A taxi driver who took me on several tours was quite unbelievably knowledgeable about Britain, our Royal Family and for some reason, Robert Burns. He was of Polynesian descent he told me, a fact which did not prepare me at all for his tendency to recite Burns's poems at great length. I have to humbly admit that his memory of these was far better than mine.

The plane landed in Sydney at 6.30am – not the best hour to meet perfect strangers who are also your employers. I need not have worried. From the moment I met these delightful people, who had arisen at dawn to greet me, I felt at ease and knew I was going to enjoy this trip very

Ye flowery banks o'bonnie Doon
How can ye blume sae fair

much indeed. I was taken to my hotel and left there for several hours, to unpack and settle in and was later taken to the kitchens of the *Australian Woman's Weekly* magazine. There I met the home economists of the magazine, including their cookery editor, who was to accompany me on my travels across Australia. Soon we were chatting as though we had known each other for years. Everything was going well – and then I had my big shock.

When I sent my recipes through to Australia, there had been no adverse comments and I knew my books sold well in that country, so assumed that we cooked in a similar manner, with due regard to the difference in the ingredients available. No one had told me about the Australian's special method and talent for icing cakes. At that time the Beatles were due to visit Australia and I was shown the cake that the magazine had prepared to greet them. This was the size of a small occasional table but what caught my eye immediately was the top of the cake. It was covered with a selection of the wild flowers of Australia, all made in icing, but of a kind of icing I had never seen before. Every petal was so fine that it looked real and the flowers were formed so perfectly you felt you could pick them. This icing bore no relation to the more formal style I knew.

I fell into a panic. 'My goodness,' I thought, 'they will expect me to do this too, and I don't know how.' Fortunately common sense prevailed. The Australian team had already seen my demonstration menus and they knew what I was going to be cooking. They *couldn't* expect me to do this! But I decided that I would learn how to do this icing before I returned home. I remember having all these thoughts while I managed to conduct a conversation and appear suitably calm and collected. I later confessed this moment of panic to some of my Australian companions: they had had no idea at the time that I had been suffering from severe fright.

The first week in Sydney was to be most exacting. I was to record several television programmes, each an hour long, and all sponsored. This was an entirely different concept of television cookery to the one I knew and entailed much planning. It was important that each sponsor had the right amount of time, that the recipes used their products wisely and would be of interest to viewers.

When I was introduced to the two home economists who were to be my assistants for this first difficult week, I realised just what careful and considerate planning had gone into arranging this part of the tour at the Australian end. Both were employed by the Sydney Gas Company, who were major sponsors. Annette was an Australian, who had spent considerable time in England, and Lesley an English girl, who had worked with the gas industry in England before settling in Australia. Naturally we had lots in common, which made an immediate bond between us.

I was asked to have my photograph taken sampling typical Australian food. I agreed of course, and then I saw the first food I was expected to eat – a plate of the famous Australian oysters. Years before I had been a great lover of oysters, but on one occasion I had eaten some and had been very ill. Since that time I hadn't touched them. Fortunately it was just before the weekend, so if I was to be ill I could suffer in solitary discomfort. Down went the oysters. Were they delicious! As I had no ill effects whatsoever, I enjoyed them throughout my time in Australia. I had them raw, as an important ingredient in **Carpet Bag Steak,** and in an unusual and luxurious **Oyster Sauce**, which turns chicken into a truly gourmet dish. As oysters are far from cheap, I have given more economical alternatives in the recipes.

After the photography session was over and we had planned the following week, I was left to left to 'find my feet' over the weekend. The editor of the magazine had invited me to lunch on the Sunday, so that was a pleasure in store. Meanwhile, I knew I would enjoy wandering around and finding out more about Sydney, which seemed busier than I had

expected. My hotel was in the centre, so I had a good chance to look at the shops and stores nearby.

My hotel room was comfortable, but very cold. I was in Australia in May, which was their winter. I had expected it to be chilly, thanks to good advice from a friend who had warned me at the last minute to take clothes suitable for a typical British winter. I was warmly clad for walking about but trying to relax in an unheated bedroom was not so easy. That night I retired early to get under the blankets.

If I had been in a hotel at home I would have requested some kind of heating but I was reminded of Bob's parting words: 'Don't be a whingeing Pom.' I felt any kind of complaint about the cold would label me as one of that despised breed; so I must endure the discomfort.

Imagine my joy when I arrived at the home of my host and hostess on the Sunday to find a glowing coal fire. 'You do have fires then?' 'Good gracious yes, haven't you a heater in your hotel bedroom?' I repeated my husband's words which were greeted with a very brisk, 'Whingeing Pom be damned – ask for a heater the moment you get back!' The porter who finally delivered this welcome article to my room was surprised: 'I thought you were used to cold houses in Britain,' he said.

On the Monday following my first weekend we started preparing for the demonstrations. These were to be recorded, but they were to run straight through if possible, so that they worked like a live programme. This pleased me very much, for nearly all the TV programmes I have presented have been live. Annette and Lesley gave wonderful support and the atmosphere in the studio was relaxed but very efficient.

I think the programmes went well – although the first one was a bit of a trial. As well as the gas company and the *Australian Woman's Weekly,* many Australian food companies and manufacturers of appliances had helped to sponsor the tour. Representatives of all these sponsoring companies were seated in a line, well within my vision. To my horror they had pens and pencils poised and throughout the recording. I could see them making notes, ticking when they felt I had described their product adequately. I found it very distracting and had to ask them to sit where I couldn't see them. By the end of that week we were all very tired, but pleasantly so. I was delighted to have a quiet dinner and an early night for I knew that the next weeks were to be very hectic indeed. I was to demonstrate to live audiences in and around Sydney, then travel to all the major cities.

When I first arrived I had been presented with the most beautiful flowers and a huge basket of typical Australian fruits – including mangoes, guavas and a fruit I had never seen before, monstera deliciosa. It was explained to me that this fruit, which has a cone-like appearance, is ready to eat when the outer rind falls away. I was just drifting off to sleep when I was awakened by a strange plop-plopping noise. What on earth could it be? Yes, it was the rind falling off my monstera deliciosa. Out of bed I jumped and, tired as I was, sat down to sample it. It was delicious, tasting like a combination of banana and pineapple. During my time in Sydney, in-between giving demonstrations, I was entertained magnificently and, from a house overlooking the harbour, I had the chance to marvel at the beautiful Sydney Harbour Bridge at night. The Sydney Opera House was not yet built, and there was still much discussion as to what its ultimate shape should be. Lottery tickets were being sold everywhere to help towards the cost of the Opera House, so whenever I see a photograph of the building, or hear of a concert being held there, I say to myself, 'Yes, Marguerite, you bought a little bit of one brick.'

I flew from Sydney to Canberra to give two demonstrations. The next day my return flight was delayed by *freezing fog* of all things! No one believed me when I told them this was very rare in Britain. Sitting waiting for the plane back to Sydney, I was approached by a man who introduced himself as Brian Epstein – the manager of the Beatles who was in Australia organizing their forthcoming tour. To my amazement he said he knew all about my appearances at the London Palladium and had even seen one. I wish I could have claimed I had been to a Beatles concert.

Sir Frank Packer, who owned the *Australian Woman's Weekly*, was abroad at the time but his sons were kind enough to host a party for me when I left Sydney to go on to Melbourne. The food in Sydney was excellent, with great emphasis placed on classic French dishes, enhanced by tropical fruits. As I expected, the meat was of superb quality – although several people were surprised when I assured them we had good meat in Britain too. The fish dishes were delicious and I tasted varieties new to me, including shark, now of course, available, if not plentiful, in Britain too. The weather was not suitable for barbecues but so many Britishers who had settled in Australia said what a joy it was to be able to plan an outdoor event in advance and be almost 100 per cent certain that the weather would be fine. Most of the cooking in hotels and restaurants was based on well-known classic dishes, with an Australian touch, and with a hint too of the exciting dishes that their new settlers, who were arriving from so many different countries, were bringing with them.

I enjoyed coffee and **Gems** – isn't that a lovely name for feather-light scones? Traditionally these are cooked in special irons in the oven, but I have experimented with baking without these and the gems are just as delicious. Annette taught me how to make the **Australian Icing** but I knew that ahead of me lay hours and hours of practice before I could achieve anything like the standard of the icing I had seen. I enjoyed sampling real **Lamingtons**: at that period tea was still an important Australian meal.

My audiences were wonderful, welcoming and full of questions. One question baffled me for a few seconds. 'How do I make a perfect Pav?' As I came from Brighton I could only associate the word Pav with our spectacular Royal Pavilion. Of course the questioner was referring to the meringue dessert, **Pavlova**.

Many of the people attending the demonstrations had come from Britain within recent years, so I was a link with home. When I finally left for home some weeks later, I was armed with addresses and requests: 'Would you drop a line please and tell my mother in Manchester, or wherever, that you have met me and that I look happy?' It was typical too, to be asked about cities and towns in Britain. Is the Music Hall Theatre still there in Aberdeen? Has Nottingham changed? etc. etc. I had to rack my brains to try and remember my last visit to the place in question and give a sensible reply. It is true to say that I met someone I had known or worked with back home in every Australian state. Suddenly, the world seemed much smaller. Australians are incredibly hospitable and I was asked over and over again if I could spare time to go to their homes for a meal or a rest.

Melbourne was lovely, an elegant and gracious city. Here again everyone from the gas company was kind and helpful. I had said farewell to both Annette and Lesley when I left New South Wales, taking with me several lovely mementos of my stay. A wonderful opal brooch and a sheet of opal set in rock and a musical Koala called Shortbread. Why Shortbread? One of the demonstration menus was not quite perfectly planned. I had to spend too much time waiting to get things into the ovens – my fault completely – and Lesley lost no time in letting me know she didn't think much of my planning. During the demonstration she hissed in my ear in far from ladylike tones: 'Get that ruddy shortbread in the oven – I can't wait any longer!'

In Melbourne I found a *real* whingeing Pom. The chambermaid in my hotel trapped me whenever she could to tell me how awful Australia was, and how she wished she was back home. On the Sunday morning I was hurrying to write a letter home, for I was being taken for a long trip in the hills behind Melbourne and then out to lunch. The chambermaid kept on, and on, so finally I put down my pen and said, 'Well, why did you leave England?' 'Because the weather was so bad.' 'Is that the only reason?' 'Yes.' It was a job to keep a straight face, because although that Sunday was beautifully fine, the weather I had suffered during my visit left a lot to be desired. I knew though that there would be wonderful summer days ahead in Melbourne and elsewhere, so simply said, 'Well the weather is just as bad in England now as when you left, so you did the right thing.'

For those who emigrated to Australia, I think the wrench from home was worse for the women of the family than the men and children, especially if they were not working. The men, when they found the jobs they wanted had companionship and interests. The children soon made friends at school and became Australians very quickly; but the mothers had time to think about all the things they had left behind – including Bramley cooking apples. If I had a pound for every person who said their apple pies were not not the same without them, I would now be rich.

After one of my demonstrations in Melbourne a pretty young woman came up to me with tears pouring down her face. 'Good Heavens,' I said 'I have never had that effect on anyone before, whatever is the matter?' 'I had never felt homesick before you mentioned watercress,' she said. I knew watercress was scarce in Australia and had simply mentioned the fact that if I had been making a certain dish at home I would have added watercress. I made a mental note not to mention it in future.

One of my cookery books, *Step-by-Step Cookery*, published by Hamlyn, had a special Australian edition, because there, as in America, there are different measures and different terms for certain foods. I left home before the first copies of this arrived, so my efficient secretary sent me a list of the main differences, so I could use the right words. When I reached Hobart in Tasmania I was getting used to calling a spring onion a 'scallion' and obviously sounded rather pompous about it. My audience was very elegant: there were plenty of white gloves and flowered hats, for demonstrations were fairly formal events in those days. A woman in the front row stood up and raised her hand (as if she were a traffic policeman), to ensure silence and stated: 'Mrs. Patten please remember there is no need to use terms like 'scallions' here. We are all very British in Tasmania and we call a spring onion a spring onion.'

I travelled to Queensland and loved Brisbane. It seemed small and cosy, for the capital of a state. I believe that it has now grown enormously. I did manage to locate one of Bob's friends from the war years here. His name was Rupert Small, but he was known as Rupert Bainbridge Small in Britain, since he thought all British people had double-barrelled names. This man, who I understood to have been a wild tearaway while in Britain was now a sophisticated and quiet dress designer.

When my hosts heard about my interest in gardening, they gave me every opportunity to visit beautiful parks and gardens. In Brisbane I was taken by a member of the gas company to a research and experimental fruit and vegetable-growing establishment, where I learned of the high regard in Australia for English strawberries and Worthing-grown tomatoes. I saw avocados, of various shapes, on the trees. When I was entertained to lunch one day I was given avocados baked around the joint of beef. My hostess asked if we did this in Britain and I explained that, while avocados were becoming more and more popular, their price did not encourage us to treat them like roast potatoes. I learned of many more ways of serving this adaptable fruit, both sweet and savoury, including a very delicious **Avocado and Lemon Soup** and Avocado Ice Cream. The ice cream is so easy to make: it is simply a blend of mashed, ripe avocados, lemon juice, whipped cream and sugar to taste.

Before I left Queensland I took a few days' holiday at Surfers' Paradise – how aptly named it is. Gloriously warm, with beautiful sandy beaches. (I hate to confess that Bondi beach, in Sydney was a little bit of a let-down. It was so much smaller than I had imagined it to be.) The days of sun in Surfers' were a joy and it was there that I discovered a wonderful home-made sweet shop. There they were – old-fashioned humbugs, coconut chips, bars of thick, nutty toffee. I went inside to marvel and buy and found the business was owned by an elderly couple who had come from Britain a few years beforehand. They were doing a roaring trade.

I was fortunate to have this chance to visit so many different places in

Australia, for the distances between the states are so large that many Australians never see the whole of their country. It was an added pleasure to be working with the people, for I learned so much more about the country and its way of life that if I had been a mere tourist.

In Adelaide I witnessed the reputed toughness of the Australians. I knew from my schedule that on one day during the time at Adelaide I was to visit another town, Whyalla. What I did not realise was that it was 250 miles from Adelaide! We had to get up at the crack of dawn to travel there because I had both an afternoon and an evening demonstration in the town. These took place in the ballroom of the hotel where we were staying. At the close of the evening session I was told, 'We are having a party, but as you have to be on the road at 6am to get back to Adelaide, you had better stay only a short time and then get to bed by midnight.' This I did, but when I came down early in the morning to join my fellow travellers back to Adelaide, they were still partying.

Just before I left Adelaide, a senior home economist who had been with me for quite a few days, said, 'Marguerite, you are so polite about everything out here – there *must* be something you think we cook badly. Come on, give me an honest answer.' To this question I replied, 'Well, why do you overcook your excellent vegetables?' A twinkle came into the woman's eyes. 'We are mainly of British stock, and we learned to over-cook vegetables from our mothers and grandmothers.' I hastened to add that in Britain we had now learned the error of our ways and were beginning to cook vegetables properly. That was only semi-true of that particular era but I'm thankful to say that even in restaurants today one expects – and generally gets – properly cooked vegetables.

One dish I had not sampled so far was kangaroo tail soup. In Adelaide the home economists cooked it for me. As this was done just before I was due to leave, I had no chance to taste it, so boarded the plane from Adelaide to Perth clutching a large jar of soup. It tasted remarkably similar to oxtail soup, with a slightly more gamey flavour.

If I ever return to Australia, and I hope I shall, I would like to begin my trip at Perth. I was getting homesick by the time I reached this city and I did not appreciate its beauties as much as I should. Apart from my time in Queensland, the bad weather had followed me all the way across Australia. In Perth the cold was combined with pouring rain, so there was little chance for sightseeing. I sympathized with the many apologies made for the weather – we know that feeling well, don't we, when our British weather lets us down? (Funnily enough my granddaughter, Joanna, spent several months in Australia a few years ago and she had just the same cold weather I experienced, so maybe we, as a family, bring it to the country.)

At the end of one of my first demonstrations in Perth, to my amazement and delight, I saw one of my colleagues from back in the Northmet, Barnet days. I had no idea Pearl had married an Australian and settled in Perth. Her husband was a surgeon and it was lovely to sit in their home and recall those far away days.

After a week in Perth it was time to leave Australia. There are so many things I shall remember about it. I have fondest memories of the people I met and worked with. They had similar ideas to me and a sense of humour very much like my friends back home. The kindness and consideration I was shown by everyone, including casual acquaintances, was unbelievable.

Many people asked me why Britain was planning to join the EEC. I felt totally inadequate to answer the questions put to me on this subject but I was aware that people felt very bitter about it. They felt that we were abandoning a country which was a fellow member of the Commonwealth and which had supported Britain in two world wars.

I am happy to say that I am still in contact with some of the people I met. The song 'I left my heart in San Francisco' is true for me – I certainly left a little bit of it there – but I left a mighty big proportion in Australia!

On my way back from Australia I was to visit Singapore and Hong Kong, spending nearly a week in each place. I arrived at the airport at Singapore, and to my astonishment, and that of my fellow travellers, we were not allowed to hail taxis. Instead we were all led to a convoy of coaches with the reassurance that we would be taken to our hotels. The illusion that all was well was shattered when we spotted soldiers with loaded guns standing at every window and entrance of each coach.

We were told then that there was so much civil unrest that this was the only safe way for us to travel. The coaches dropped everyone off but it was dark and I couldn't see anything of Singapore or gauge how the local population was behaving.

At the hotel we was ordered to stay inside until we were given the all-clear. That sounded very grim – I could be trapped inside a hotel for nearly a week. So much for all my plans to sample the various cuisines of this country. I knew it was a meeting place of a great many different cultures – Chinese, Indian, Malaysian – and I had been looking forward to sampling a variety of dishes. My other ambition was to visit the world-famous hotel – Raffles. I knew it was near my own hotel, for we had dropped several passengers off there on the way. It looked *so* interesting. Would I be able to walk round there? 'No!' I was told, so I sat down with a book to relax as best I could.

The telephone rang in my room. It was the airline, who told me they could get me a passage to Hong Kong the very next day. They suggested this would be a much better idea than waiting for the curfew to be lifted. I agreed. The next morning as I was leaving the hotel, in a coach without guards, I heard that everything had returned to normal. Too late! I had been to Singapore – and left it – without seeing anything at all. I never found out exactly what had been going on, but knew the unrest was between the Chinese and Malaysian populations. The following year, 1965, Singapore became independent.

At least I had had an interesting dinner in my hotel the night before. The menu I was handed first was truly international. It looked excellent but consisted of the kind of dishes available in large hotels all over the world. I managed to persuade the waiter to bring me the menu for 'locals'. I started with Bird's Nest Soup, which was so much better than any I had tasted at Chinese restaurants in Britain. Then I selected **Pork** with a truly delicious **Satay Sauce**. **Toffee Apples** and refreshing cups of China tea, ended a very pleasant meal.

Hong Kong was sheer delight from beginning to end. I had been told in Australia, that there were plans for me to do a certain amount of television while I was there and I was to be met and shown around the city. Unfortunately, these television programmes never happened. Owing to the exceptionally high humidity at the time, a number of programmes were dropped, cookery among them, so I really was on holiday.

The meals I had were simply splendid. They often just consisted of one beautifully cooked dish, rather than the mixture of dishes we expect from a Chinese menu. Up until that time I had never liked ginger in any form, but when I tasted the **Fish in Sesame and Ginger** I was converted. It was made with snapper, but it is also excellent cooked with any firm-textured fish. **Lemon Chicken** is a wonderful combination of sharp lemon juice and chicken. I like to make this with a large chicken. Any left is wonderful served cold.

In the sixties we were far less used to using a combination of sweet and savoury flavours than we are today, so I was intrigued to sample sweet and sour fish. The combination of ingredients in **Sweet and Sour Pork with Water Chestnuts** can be adapted for fish and other sweet and sour dishes.

My memories of Hong Kong are still so vivid and so pleasant. I was taken around and entertained and I also wandered by myself through the busy streets, marvelling at the bustling atmosphere. I bought some small gifts but nothing of great value because I was so overwhelmed by the selection of goods on offer that I couldn't decide where to begin! Everyone who has been to Hong Kong for however short a time will agree that it is an Aladdin's cave. There is so much to see, to buy and to eat.

Perhaps my most lasting memory is of the smiling faces of the children. The tiny boys and girls are exquisite. I would often see a child, not much more than a toddler, in charge of one or more even smaller infants - all of them beaming away at me. One day I visited a beautiful garden that was open to the public and was talking to some small children when a voice, with a distinct American accent said, 'Lady, be careful! They're after your money. They weren't. They were simply anxious for me to hear just how well they spoke English.

The final leg of my journey home took me through Delhi — where at the airport in the dead of night I managed to buy Judith a traditional Indian doll to add to her collection – and Thailand and Greece, where we stopped to re-fuel. Finally we landed, absolutely on time, at Heathrow. It had been a wonderful trip, but the best part was the greeting given me by Bob and Judith. I had left on a hot day in May and returned on an equally sunny morning in August. Britain looked at its best.

CHAPTER 8

International Inspiration

I n August, 1964, after I returned from my long trip to Australia there were several busy weeks, catching up with various jobs. There were articles to be written and letters to friends and relations telling them all the news. Everyone had been so helpful and efficient in my absence that nothing had gone wrong at all.

After this fairly brief period, though, Bob and I were ready for a holiday. We were going to Morocco, a country Bob had never visited although Judith and I had holidayed there in 1963. On that occasion our hotel in Tangier was immaculate, the rooms delightful and our first dinner a real feast. On the first evening we were treated to a wonderful spectacle. A baby son had been born to King Hassan and the whole of Morocco was celebrating this event. Past the hotel came horsemen, all in their Arab robes, with flaming torches held high. We felt as though we were part of the *Arabian Nights*. My love of this country began at that moment. I was only too pleased to be going again with Bob.

I loved visiting the market, and never have I seen more splendid produce: the fruits and vegetables we associate with tropical climates nestled beside excellent strawberries, apples and pears and more homely potatoes and salad ingredients. The flowers were delightful too.

There are many foreign influences in Tangier, which had been under direct Moroccan rule only since 1956 – from 1923 until that date it had been a neutral, international zone. The links with European countries, especially France and Spain, are reflected in the diversity of restaurants and foods where classic European dishes are served side by side with Moroccan specialities. We learned the art of bargaining, sipping delicious mint tea with the shopkeepers and enjoying a leisurely discussion about the price of the goods we wanted to buy.

On other visits we rented a villa. Judith and I were once fortunate enough to be invited to the pre-wedding celebrations of the bride at the home of our next-door neighbours. The bride-to-be looked exquisite and so did her friends. We were initiated into the dances and songs. Great platters of small **Almond Biscuits**, in various shapes, and bite-sized **Sweet B'stillas** (delicate pastry filled with ground almonds and cinnamon) were served throughout the evening.

A journalist friend, who lived in Tangier, taught me how to prepare **Kababs** (cubes of meat, known as Kebabs in other Middle Eastern countries) so as to give them their subtle, spiced flavour, before being cooked on skewers. I also learned a new way of cooking **Fish with Dates**.

Tangier is full of interesting and unusual residents. We met and become friends with Lily – no-one ever called her anything else – who owned a very special bar there. When she died several years ago her passing was recorded at great length in a British newspaper. Lily joined us on one of our trips to a small seaside resort nearby, where we chased our lunch on the beach. Crabs and lobsters rushed in all directions – we simply pointed to the one that took our fancy, went for a long stroll along the sands, and returned an hour or so later to sit down to delicious seafood salad.

On Bob's first visit to Tangier with me he returned to the hotel one night having met a wealthy local resident. He told Bob that every Sunday he ate boiled beef and dumplings for lunch – odd in a hot country where local dishes were so exciting and exotic. Apparently it had been his special favourite when was a long-term guest of Her Majesty in Dartmoor Prison. He was not, I believe, the only resident with a shady past.

While staying in Marrakech one year, Bob nearly found himself a job. It was a time when Polaroid cameras were far less widely known than they are today and he was enjoying himself taking instant photographs of the people and picturesque scenery. He took a picture of a man who owned camels for people to hire and presented it to him. The excitement! Immediately Bob was invited inside the man's home to take pictures of the family and then asked if he would stay on over the holiday period to take pictures of the tourists. The money he – the camel dealer – and Bob – the photographer – would make together!

It was when we left Marrakech for Rabat, one of the most interesting and elegant places in Morocco, that our real adventure began. En route, our car developed a faint smell of burning. We were not unduly worried at first but suddenly it was on fire! I began hauling cases from the car and Bob found a blanket in the boot and crawled underneath the car to try and extinguish the flames. Happily he succeeded. Anyone who has been to Morocco knows how a crowd can gather in a matter of minutes, seemingly out of nowhere. On this occasion a group soon surrounded us with everyone giving good advice. We were rescued by a man driving a dustcart, who took me to our hotel in Rabat to find professional help. The story ended happily and we continued to enjoy the atmosphere and the food of this fascinating country.

Over the years I learned to make a really good **Couscous**, the national

dish. This is based on semolina and it can be varied in many ways – served with chicken or meat or vegetables and always combined with some fruits and served with a hot, spiced sauce. The **Orange Salads** of various kinds are a wonderful way to begin a meal and if you are tired of ordinary roast chicken, do try **Chicken with Olives and Lemons** or **Djaja Mammra**, in which the chicken is stuffed with almonds, raisins and semolina. I have always liked demonstrating couscous, for at the mention of semolina a strangely glazed look comes over the faces of my audience as they conjure u childhood memories of a much-hated sticky pudding served with jam or fruit. But the semolina in couscous is quite different.

The savoury or sweet **Tajines,** in which the food is cooked so slowly, are a joy to eat. As well as being the name of a stew, the word *tajine* also describes the earthenware dish in which it is cooked in Morocco. It has a fascinating conical lid with a hole in it. The hole allows excess steam to escape during cooking. My recipe at the back uses an ordinary casserole, which works very well.

I have also picked up some lovely recipes in Holland. In the early 1970s I was invited by the Dutch branch of the Electrical Association for Women to give a large demonstration to some hundreds of people to celebrate their 21st anniversary.

It was too tempting. It was spring and I was told that after the hard work would come my treat. I would be taken to see the wonderful bulb fields. As an enthusiastic gardener, how could I refuse?

A Dutch home economist came to England to help with the arrangements. As it was to be such a special demonstration, she wanted the dishes to come from around the world. To add to the festive atmosphere each finished dish would be shown to the audience by someone wearing the costume of the relevant country.

On the evening before the demonstration I was taken to an Indonesian restaurant where I came to appreciate the close links between Holland and its previous colonies. The food was excellent and I was glad to have the opportunity to sample an authentic nasi goreng, that delicious mixture of rice, fish and meat. Beforehand I had **Gulai Ikan**, fish cooked with spices in coconut milk. This is excellent with many different kinds of fish and a splendid way of turning canned tuna into an interesting dish.

The demonstration was interesting from my point of view, for everything I said had to be translated into Dutch: I had to adapt my actions – creaming, beating, etc. – to the tempo of the translator's words. I am sorry that I have never had a chance to do this again. It is a fascinating exercise.

I learned one important cookery skill in Holland. After the demonstration we ate small cocktail 'bites' before the meal and one of the dishes served were tiny meatballs, known as **Fricadeller**. They were especially delicious because they were very soft and delicate inside and I couldn't understand how this had been done. My Dutch home economist friend explained that they added a little gelatine to the meat mixture. This set the ingredients, so they were easy to handle. During cooking the gelatine melts: hence the moist texture. Why hadn't I thought of that?

The bulbs were, as I had expected, quite breathtaking. At teatime before my departure I sampled the famous **Dutch Apple Cake**, an interesting alternative to our traditional recipes.

Anyone who cooks must appreciate just how much we owe the French chefs of the past, and present, for all they have taught us about classic cooking. No matter what fashions in food come and go it is essential to use a good balance of ingredients, especially when baking, and it is this skill I have learned from the French masters.

France is such a large country that the cooking of each area cannot be summed up as 'traditionally French'. Personally, I have a great fondness for the food of Normandy and the more sophisticated cuisine of Paris. Some years ago *Woman's Own*, the magazine for whom I was cookery consultant at the time, opened a cookery school at Deauville. On a cold

January day, Jane Reed, who was then the editor of the magazine, and I went out to France for the opening of the school. We spent the first week there, joining in the classes with the pupils. These were conducted very skilfully by two local chefs who included specialities of Normandy in their demonstrations.

I do get exasperated though with people who say: 'All the French are good cooks', or, 'You never have a bad meal in France'. That is just *not* true. I have had excellent food there, but I have also had indifferent food.

For many years we had a holiday home in Provence in the south of France. We did not have a villa, but invested in two mobile homes – the name given to large and civilised caravans. When I say 'civilized' I mean equipped with hot and cold water, refrigerators and good cooking facilities, plus comfortable beds. It was a sudden decision to buy them and it was prompted by the fact that they were situated in a pine wood and I could create an attractive garden around them. At first I was not sure whether I was going to enjoy this gypsy-like existence but I became the greatest lover of our yearly months in that beautiful part of the world. It was a sad blow when the land was sold for development; the informal and relaxed way of life was very special.

When we first arrived in Provence in 1976, I decided that I would hardly cook at all and that the family would eat out as much as possible. 'I am on holiday,' I stated firmly. But I found that although the shops and markets were full of the most wonderful produce, it rarely seemed to reach the restaurants. And I had longed to become an expert in Provençal cooking and had thought I had the perfect opportunity to learn. Year after year we tried different places to eat. There was nothing wrong with the quality of the food, it was just so dull. The choice of vegetables in most restaurants, both inexpensive and more luxurious, was very simple: *pommes frites* and *haricots verts*. Sadly the haricot beans were not always green – on the contrary they were often greyish and obviously out of a can. I smile when people tell me how much the British love chips. The French could match us chip for chip any time!

To be fair, some of the restaurants are open only for the summer season and have make their income then, but, with a few exceptions, even those that are open all year round are disappointing.

There is one superb restaurant at least in St. Tropez: 'des Mouscardins'. Before our first year in Provence we were having a meal in The Black Lion, a local restaurant in Brighton which no longer exists, where we knew the staff well. One of the waiters told us he was leaving to work for a member of his family who had a restaurant in St. Tropez. We promised to visit him there.

We found the place, read the bill of fare, and saw that the meals looked wonderful, but very costly. Finances were tight because in those days travellers abroad were only allowed to take a very limited amount of money out of Britain. Jean-Claude greeted us with great enthusiasm: we were the first British people to have visited him. We had a wonderful meal, choosing expensive items to give ourselves a treat, and then found we were not to be presented with a bill. Fortunately, we have been able to repay our friend's hospitality on other occasions.

While eating out may be a risk, cooking in Provence has always been a delight. In our local butchers there was an excellent charcuterie section with cooked meats and ready-prepared salads – ideal for lazy holidays. Fresh vegetables, salads and fruits were available in great abundance too. And these days you can get excellent wholemeal bread as well as delicious traditional loaves.

There are many dishes I shall associate with holiday times in France. Two of the less usual are **Fried Stuffed Avocados** (when you cut into the fruit it is full of a piping hot dressing) and the plump, garlic-flavoured **Escargots** baked in slices of French bread. The various patés are too numerous to mention but one small restaurant in the country offered delicious **Rillettes** which I have adapted so that it can be made quickly.

We no longer have a holiday home in France but I know that I, like all the family, look back over wonderfully relaxed and happy days spent in that beautiful part of the world.

Early in 1981 I was surprised to receive a letter from South Africa asking me to undertake a tour of cookery demonstrations over there. I knew no one in that country and the letter had come from an unknown source – an Afrikaans magazine called *Sarie*.

The visit was to take place in the autumn, which was some months ahead, so there was plenty of time to make arrangements. My husband and an assistant could travel with me if I wished. My daughter Judith happened to be at home when the letter arrived. Could she please be my assistant? 'But you are so busy,' I said. 'Not too busy for *that*!' she replied.

Bob had been in South Africa for a brief period during the war, and had told me how beautiful it was. Since then we had often talked about the possibility of going there for a holiday, but we had never managed it.

I accepted and Judith came with me. Bob, sadly, could not come owing to other commitments. The letters about the foods I would use, the dishes I would demonstrate and the audiences I would meet, came thick and fast. It felt strange knowing that I would not be able to check the recipes in the magazine as they would be in Afrikaans.

We arrived in Johannesburg airport and were whisked off to Pretoria to arrange the first demonstration. Afterwards there was a formal lunch and Judith and I moved from table to table, meeting and talking to our audience. This was an excellent opportunity for us to see a new country and meet new people. Indeed the whole trip was a great pleasure.

Judith and I had decided before we left England that political matters were not to be discussed. We were there to do a specific job, which we would carry out to the best of our ability. Obviously, like most people, we had our own opinions about the situation in the country and we were anxious to observe matters at first hand. Our audiences were all-white. Although they were Afrikaans, they all spoke fluent English.

The cookery editor and other members of the *Sarie* staff did all they could to make it a memorable, as well as a busy, trip. I lunched with home economists in Cape Town and compared notes on the way we worked. I visited a most interesting cookery school in the city and came away from there with a wonderful bouquet of flowers, made in the same kind of icing as used in Australia. It still holds pride of place in a cabinet in the dining-room at home.

I was given an interesting selection of books about the country and its food and customs, which have given me much pleasure. I learned how to make authentic **Bobotie** and **Bredie,** two delicious meat dishes. I was also introduced to **Sweet Potato and Apple Bake** by a delightful home economist. It is Sonnie's recipe I give at the back, with my thanks. Unfortunately, Sonnie died recently: she was a wonderful lady.

As a relaxation from the busy schedule we were taken to spend several days at Mala Mala, the game reserve. What a joy to see the animals in such natural surroundings. I shall always treasure the picture of a lioness with her cubs, relaxing in the sun, and a huge lion dozing some yards away. One cub strayed towards him and immediately the lioness put out a huge paw to stop it. You could imagine what she was saying: 'Don't you dare disturb your father when he is having his after-dinner nap.' My last demonstration was at Stellenbosch, just outside Cape Town. Here I saw the wonderful botanical gardens and also toured around the private gardens, which were full of exotic blooms. How I envied the gardeners their wonderful climate! We lunched out-of-doors and as a farewell all the guests sang their national songs.

I have recently been invited to several of South African wine-tasting sessions. It is always a pleasure to renew my acquaintance with some of the excellent wines I tasted when I was there. I particularly enjoy the wines from the Stellenbosch area.

I am sure anyone who has visited South Africa and marvelled at its beauty must wish the country a happy and secure future.

No book could allow me sufficient space to record all the varied and unusual dishes I have been able to sample during my travels for work and for pleasure, but some of the following will always be favourites of mine.

On one of the hottest days I remember, in Cyprus, I had a wonderfully refreshing meal – each course just right for the day. I began with **Iced Cucumber Soup** and followed this with an interesting chicken salad, with just a hint of curry in the creamy dressing. It was served with **Imam Bayeldi** (a piquant mixture of aubergines, garlic and tomatoes). I decided I had eaten more than enough but the sight of the **Fresh Figs in Ouzo** was too tempting to refuse.

On one holiday to Italy, I took my granddaughter, Joanna, just 10 years old at the time. A niece of mine, Vibeke Moen, reading medicine at Padua, acted as our guide. She showed us the marvels of Venice and Florence and showed us round the University of Padua. We enjoyed the most excellent food in the various hotels and restaurants and it was lovely to be so spoiled. However, when I saw the wonderful fruit and vegetable market in Padua I longed to buy the produce and start cooking. I am a great lover of globe artichokes and there were great piles of them in the market. I found the trimmed, fresh artichoke bottoms, so young and tender, particularly interesting. Joanna enjoyed the holiday as much as I did and acquitted herself well as she turned and twisted the long strands of pasta with the expertise of a true Italian. She said her mother made her practise at home before she left! It is interesting how the British are at long last appreciating the value of pasta and how highly rated it is as a healthy food.

It is also a joy to be able to buy *arborio* rice now so that you can make **Risotto** with a true creamy texture.

Spanish food is colourful and exotic, just like its people, which is perhaps is why it is so popular with the British. If I were asked to select just one Spanish dish from the many I love it would be **Gazpacho.** I never understand why this is not served more often, for in hot weather it is the ideal start to a meal. Cold soups are just as delicious as piping hot ones.

My sister, Elizabeth, still lives in Norway and I have visited her there, and taken in Denmark and Sweden, on a number of occasions. Elizabeth has always given me most helpful information about Norwegian foods and made sure I have sampled their special delicacies.

If I were asked to sum up on what Scandinavian cooking has taught me, I would say that it was the presentation of food. Every dish served is presented beautifully, often with an attractive garnish or decoration.

The term 'open sandwiches' sounds very simple doesn't it? Surely, all you do is put food on to slices of bread and butter. This hardly describes *smorrebrod.* The true open sandwiches of Denmark, which are almost as popular in Norway, with their clever combination of flavours, colours and textures, are a pleasure to behold – and to eat.

Some of my happiest times in Norway have been when attending the confirmation of my two nieces. These were times of family celebration, with each guest bringing a poem in honour of the person being confirmed. The Norwegian cold table is at its most impressive at such an event. I love their light-as-a-feather **Blötkake** (layer cake) and the wide selection of crisp, sweet biscuits. Another cake I now make for special occasions consists of almond rings forming a tower, known as a **Kransekake**. This is traditionally served in Norway at Christmas time, but it is an impressive cake for any time of the year.

During a family holiday in Denmark, we met an exceptionally interesting man, Teddy Barritt, the manager of a hotel bar in Copenhagen. He spoke perfect English – not surprising, as his father was British. Before the Second World War, and for a time during the war years, Teddy had owned a famous restaurant in Copenhagen, called Scotties. Among his clients had been many members of the German Reichbank, some of whom still patronized it during the German occupation of Denmark. They must have had an inkling that Teddy was a member of the Danish resistance movement and so he took great risks. One of his customers – a German – warned him that his life was in danger and told him to escape. He did, just in time, and went to Sweden in the hold of a Swedish fishing boat. When he took Bob on a tour of Copenhagen, Bob said people stopped to shake Teddy by the hand. Even a policeman held up the traffic to do so – Teddy was considered a true Danish hero.

I remember one particular Danish meal very well: I had roast wild duck with the most delicious **Beetroot and Apple Salad**, followed by **Rice Almond Pudding** (which is originally a Norwegian dish). If you usually find rice pudding dull, try it – it may well make you change your mind.

For a quite different cuisine, with a true Mediterranean touch, Bob and I enjoyed a holiday touring Portugal. We were there several weeks and all the fish and much of the other food we sampled was delicious. Our great discovery was **Fresh Sardines** which we tasted in Cascais, near Estoril, where they were caught and cooked by the locals. We so enjoyed sitting outdoors in the evening, enjoying the warm sun and our delicious freshly caught meal.

I hope the years ahead will offer me many more opportunities to travel and to learn about the foods, dishes and customs of many countries. It is the greatest pleasure to me.

CHAPTER 9

And Now...

'When are you going to retire?' is a question I am frequently asked. The answer is, 'When I am no longer fit enough to work and I stop enjoying what I'm doing.' And I do *enjoy* my work so much. Everything I am asked to do is both a pleasure and a challenge. It means I work hard, but at something I love. I hope I am not tempting providence when I say that I am extremely healthy.

Some of my time these days is spent keeping up-to-date with the world of food and nutrition. It has changed so much during recent years and I have to know the latest facts, theories and fashions. I am a Fellow of the Cookery and Food Association, a Member of the Guild of Food Writers and also a member of the Forum on Food and Health at the Royal Society of Medicine. In this latter capacity I learn the medical facts about the food we eat and the way it affects our health. I am not over-fond of health experts and journalists who wag their fingers and warn us about what we shouldn't eat without offering plenty of positive facts and interesting recipes. This attitude gives the us the idea that we either eat food we enjoy, which is bad for us; or eat food that does us good, but which we dislike. This is quite wrong. Meals should be enjoyable *and* nutritious.

The great talking point of today is the British diet and how we should cut down on fat. Some experts and health writers hark back to the British wartime diet and state that we were healthier then than we are now. Of course, with the rations we were allowed in those days, it *was* impossible to overdose on fat, sugar and meat. And we had to make the best use of the limited range of fresh vegetables and fruits with flour and oats to 'fill the gaps'. There were no between-meal snacks as there are today. But who would really want to go back to those days of deprivation? Today we have such a wonderful choice of delicious, healthy ingredients in our shops that it *should* be easy to eat wisely.

There have been various trends in cooking and food presentation during the past years. One contentious fashion is *nouvelle cuisine,* a style often mocked because some restaurants used it as an excuse to serve tiny portions of food at a very high price. But the idea behind this new look at classic cooking – which now includes *cuisine naturelle* – is a very good one. It is that you don't mask the flavour of fresh ingredients with over-rich sauces or over-elaborate decoration but strive to serve each ingredient so that it retains the maximum natural flavour. What could be better?

The move towards vegetarian meals is interesting. When I first began cooking, the range of vegetarian dishes was limited and vegetarians were regarded as cranks. Pulses (peas, beans and lentils) were described as *second-class* proteins. We know now that there is nothing second class about them and that they, together with a wide range of other non-meat foods available today, mean that vegetarian dishes are varied and delicious. Neither my husband nor I are vegetarians but I frequently include non-meat dishes in our menus, including the **Lentil and Bean Stir-Fry,** which you will find at the back.

I enjoy the less rigid menu planning of today – why not serve cheese as a first course, as in **Pear and Walnut Salad** (which includes smoked cheese), or small portions of poultry or game before a main course of fish, as in **Spiced Quail** and **Duck with Apple Coulis**? Our relatively recent rediscovery of herbs would delight our ancestors.

We are now a nation of wine-drinkers and appreciate the value of wine not only as an accompaniment to a meal, but also in cooking. We are not afraid to sample unknown names. It is fascinating to find out about the wines from different countries, as each reflects something of the particular area in which the vines are grown. Our choice of foods and wines and our ever-changing world of cookery is exciting for everyone, including food writers. I hope I can continue to meet this challenge.

I find it interesting that Britain, which has always considered itself so conservative in its choice of food, has now embraced a variety of raw ingredients and dishes that cover the cuisines of the world. This is not only due to the ethnic minorities that have settled in this country and created a market for their national produce, but also to the many specialist restaurants that allow us to 'eat our way around the world', and to the fact that so many people holiday abroad in exotic countries.

Books and TV programmes have played their part too. It's not so long ago that I introduced dishes from other countries into my demonstrations with caution. I remember demonstrating a risotto to an audience during the sixties. The only way I could lure them into accepting it with any degree of enthusiasm was by declaring that it was the Italian equivalent of shepherd's pie and a splendid way to use up leftover foods. Today, most adults and children are well acquainted with pizzas and pasta dishes with their various sauces, as well as Chinese and Indian dishes.

All of this adds wonderful variety to our meals, but we should remember that Britain has its own tradition of good cooking. I hope that it won't sink forever beneath our enthusiasm for ever new and more exotic tastes.

I am often asked if I disapprove of the many convenience foods now available in the shops. Of course, the term 'convenience food' is a bit of a misnomer. These vary in quality, food value and interest. After all, the vast range of cheeses, breads and cooked meats on the market can be called convenience foods. But as for ready-made dishes – I do not disapprove. I would much rather that a busy woman or man with a job, a home and a hungry family waiting for an evening meal, bought a ready-made supper when necessary than become harassed and overworked. But I hope, when time permits, that she or he will experiment with cooking home-made dishes. They are better nutritionally and cheaper than the ready-made variety. And cooking *can* be an enjoyable and relaxing occupation.

I am a great believer in using labour-saving appliances, but not fussy gadgets. I can see no virtue in grating, chopping and beating ingredients if an electric mixer or food processor will do this for you – what a joy to prepare soups and purées in a matter of seconds! It *is* a good idea, though, to know the most efficient way to chop and cut foods by hand, just in case you are left without these appliances. Like most cooks, my knives are my favourite tools, and I always tuck one or two in my luggage when I am working away from home. Freezers are a wonderful asset too, allowing us to plan ahead for special occasions or busy periods.

I have used microwave cookers both in my own home and in demonstrations for many years. People need to know how to use these useful appliances properly and how to assess their real value in the kitchen. That's why I became the Chairman of the Education Committee of the Microwave Association. (I was later made President.) A microwave is a valuable extra heating appliance in the kitchen and there are many foods that are suitable for cooking by this method. It is invaluable to busy people and, if used according to the manufacturers' instructions and with common sense, a very safe way of cooking. I know from my experience of working with the blind, that a great many blind people find their microwave has made catering a much easier task.

Many years ago I took part in special shows for large audiences in which cooking, good health and beauty care were combined. The beauty part of the session was given by Eve Gardiner, who worked for Max Factor.

I discovered that Eve also worked with the blind. She had been asked by the Government some years beforehand to teach blind girls and women how to look after their skins and apply make-up, for this played a great part in raising their morale. It was a very tough job but Eve taught herself to teach her students by making up her own face in a darkened room. She asked me to do some cookery talks for the blind. I was very nervous at the time, being completely untrained for such a job. Eve suggested that I work blindfolded at first so I could appreciate the difficulties faced by blind cooks who could see neither the ingredients nor the utensils. Over the years I have learned that little daunts blind people, many of whom enjoy cooking. Sadly, Eve Gardiner died after a long illness in 1992, but through her I have kept up my interest in working with blind people. I am now a Trustee of Soundaround, a charity founded in 1985 by Nigel Verbeek, an experienced media man who became blind in his thirties. *Soundaround* is a monthly, 90-minute sound magazine on cassette and is circulated free to visually handicapped people.

Soundaround is a brilliant concept. The cassettes – which include news, current affairs, features on gardening, make-up and cooking, competitions, quizzes and lots more – are sent out to Soundaround's listeners and returned after use. Listeners are encouraged to tape their own features and interesting tit-bits of information on these tapes and then Nigel edits the new material for the next edition. I record cookery hints and recipes each month for Soundaround and as usual have learnt so much from the information sent in to me. We run cookery competitions too, and the standard of cooking is extremely high. I am extremely proud of my association with this charity.

A few months ago I helped on a large-print cookbook for the partially sighted, prepared by the company Van den Berghs, with the approval and advice of the Royal National Institute for the Blind. Some of the money raised by the sale of the books went to this important charity. I am now preparing the scripts of cookery books on cassette for the blind, sponsored by Van den Berghs.

I also write regularly for two magazines, *Saga* and *Yours*, both of which are mainly for older people. In 1990 and 1991 *Saga* ran two cookery schools for the over-60s at the University of Dundee and I was delighted to be involved in these. Sadly, many people do become less agile, both mentally and physically, as they become older and they need all the help, companionship and understanding we can give them. However, I can say that some of my elderly students and readers are very lively and absolutely on the ball – it so infuriates me when older people are treated as if they are incompetent and helpless.

Each week I contribute a cookery page to *Argus Woman*, the magazine in my local newspaper, the *Evening Argus*. This paper covers a wide area around Brighton and has a large readership.

For many years, putting on special presentations, speaking at various conferences and lecturing in colleges have been part of my working life. I used to lecture to young home economics students, not just on cookery but also on fabric care. With new fabrics coming on to the market all the time, not to mention new laundry appliances and washing products, I found this a very absorbing subject.

I am delighted that degree courses are established so firmly for home economists. For far too long it was believed that home economics – or domestic science, as it used to be called – was a good choice for a nice, domesticated person of no great academic ability. The range of subjects covered in modern courses disproves this theory entirely. When they leave college, home economists work in many different roles. Some students are disappointed that, with so many other things in the syllabus, there is less time given to cookery, needlecraft and other practical subjects. I point out that once you have the theoretical knowledge it is possible to become expert in craftwork with practice. All over the country there are splendid evening classes given by gifted teachers. I love to work with young people and am currently a Director of Eastbourne School of Food and Fashion. I enjoy seeing these bright young girls achieve their excellent standard of cookery and needlework.

Since *Cookery in Colour* was published in 1960 (*see* Chapter 6), I have written many articles and cookery books – 157 so far. (I am told that my books have sold over 16½ million copies worldwide.) This means continually testing recipes and trying out new foods.

I realise that my greatest good fortune has been in my family. I grew up in a loving home and have had one ever since. Our only daughter, Judith, has given us nothing but pleasure and pride. I remember when she was about 15 years old she asked me, 'When do I get to the difficult age?' She never *has* reached it, I am thankful to say. I travelled a good deal, giving demonstrations around Britain when Judith was growing up and I cannot thank Bob enough for the way he helped me during those years and the encouragement he has given me throughout our marriage.

Judith now has a successful and happy career with her own public relations firm. She is a most caring and generous person, always mindful of our welfare. She has a wonderful relationship with her two children, Charles and Joanna. Like most grandparents, Bob and I think our grandchildren are very special people. We have been able to see a good deal of them, especially when they joined us for holidays in France. Like my busy mother, Judith has always made time to be with them when needed. Although divorced from her first husband, Andrew, we have all remained good friends, which has been very important to the family. When Judith married Michael our family was enlarged by her two step-children – Sue and Robert. It is a great pleasure to have them in our family and they join in all our celebrations. My brother Philip, who has retired from being a Trinity House pilot, and sister Elizabeth, have happy families too, so we are all very fortunate. Elizabeth is like me: she loves her work, so continues to teach English in Norway to a wide range of people from new entrants in the Norwegian Foreign Office to tax officials, oil executives and members of Interpol.

I love my garden in Brighton. Over the years we have established good-sized trees and shrubs, although many of the original trees had to be cut down to accommodate the house. I am often asked whether I grow vegetables, but I don't. I simply don't have the time to look after them and I would rather have a pretty garden, with plenty of flower beds, than a useful one. But I do grow herbs – like many people today I know they can work magic in cooking!

I cannot write about family life without mentioning our love of cats, for they have been an essential part of our home, giving us great affection and pleasure. Many years ago one of these cats – a large creature known as George — was responsible for my experimenting with desserts based on baked custards. Hence the recipes for **Crème Brulée** and **Brazilian Cream**. Our two cats had been ill, and the vet suggested that baked custard might tempt them to eat. They were so weak I had to feed them with teaspoons. To the end of his days George was a baked custard addict. He insisted that he sat on my lap and ate it from a spoon.

Our various Siamese cats have been a joy and over the years we have learnt to understand the way they talk. But our most intelligent cat was a perfectly ordinary tabby from the Cat Rescue Organization. He had been badly abused and someone had cut his tail off. Even the vet doubted whether he would settle, he seemed so difficult. Within a relatively short time, however, he became an affectionate nurse to an elderly cat we also had at the time and later a nursemaid to Siamese kittens, teaching them to climb, and chastizing them when they behaved badly. He seemed to know every word we said to him. Charlie was a very special cat.

Apart from gardening I still love the theatre, but it is opera that has given me the greatest pleasure over the years. I can't sing at all though. Am I disappointed not to have made a career on the stage? Not in the slightest. I still give demonstrations from time to time and love my audience and the personal contact I have with them.

I do have one disappointment, however. About 20 years ago I decided I wanted to learn to fly a plane. I had a number of lessons at Shoreham Airport, but I gave these up because I was never quite brave enough to fly solo, and it annoys me that I never completed the course. Perhaps I am the kind of person who should always have her feet on the ground.

To all my family and friends I say 'thank you' for giving me such a happy existence.

My
Favourite
Recipes

*The recipes in this book are very special. I
have chosen them because they reflect and
remind me of various periods in my life,
which I have described in the previous pages,
and they are for dishes I particularly enjoy
cooking and eating. I hope they will bring you
as much pleasure as they have me.*

*A few of the dishes date back to the era
when British cooks had to cope with rationing
and a limited range of foods; so originally
they were rather spartan. Today there are so
many more ingredients available to us, and I
have adapted the recipes accordingly.*

NOTES ON THE RECIPES

*All dishes serve four people, unless stated to the contrary.
*In a few recipes you will find less usual metric weights given, e.g. 110 g rather than 100 g as the equivalent of 4 oz. The 110 g is more accurate.
*Spoon measures are level. In a few recipes the word *level* is stressed. This is because a more generous amount could spoil the dish.
*A British tablespoon measure is equivalent to a metric 15 ml spoon.
*I have stressed that freshly ground pepper should be used. All spices deteriorate with storage and pepper is no exception. For preference purchase a pepper mill and peppercorns and grind pepper as and when required. In one or two recipes I specify 'white pepper'. This is because black pepper would spoil the colour of the dish.
*In many recipes I refer to fruit zest, rather than fruit rind. This is because it is important that none of the white pith of the citrus fruit is included, just the coloured part, with its oils and flavour.
*Ingredients are given in the order of preparation, so if a salad dressing comes before the main ingredients it is because it should be ready first.

For American readers:
*Self-raising flour is the equivalent of all-purpose flour, sifted with baking powder, see comments on page 167.
*An American tablespoon measure equals1$\frac{1}{2}$ British tablespoons.
*An American cup measure equals 250 ml or 8 fl oz of liquid.
*When measuring solid ingredients 1 American cup equals:
  100 or 110 g/4 oz plain (all-purpose) flour or a generous 110 g/4$\frac{1}{2}$ oz cornflour (cornstarch)
  225 g/8 oz butter or other fats (shortenings). (Two American spoon measures equals 25 g/1 oz fat)
  225 g/8 oz caster or granulated sugar, firmly packed; slightly less brown sugar and just over 110 g/4$\frac{1}{2}$ oz sifted icing (confectioners') sugar
  350 g/12 oz preserves or 325 g/11 oz syrups such as black treacle (molasses) or golden (corn) syrup
  150 to 175 g/5 to 6 oz dried fruits, such as currants, raisins, sultanas (seedless white raisins)
  200 g/7 oz long grain rice or 85 g/3 oz rolled oats
  100 g/4 oz grated Cheddar type cheese or 175 g/6 oz finely grated Parmesan cheese. 100 g/4 oz dried breadcrumbs or 50 g/2 oz soft breadcrumbs.

HORS D'OEUVRE

The first course of a meal is very important – it should be a pleasant introduction to the foods that follow. Over the years, our choice of hors d'oeuvre has become more adventurous; we now accept the fact that cheese, as in the recipe below, is excellent at the start of the meal.

Pear and Walnut Salad

Fresh dessert pears blend well with smoked hams, such as Parma ham, or with shellfish, such as prawns. They are also very good with smoked cheese, as in this recipe.

For the dressing:
1 teaspoon Dijon mustard
1 tablespoon walnut oil
2 tablespoons sunflower oil
1½ tablespoons lemon juice
salt and freshly ground black pepper
1 teaspoon sugar
2 tablespoons chopped walnuts, use skinned
  fresh nuts when available

4 small or 2 large ripe, but firm, dessert pears
225 to 300 g/8 to 10 oz smoked cheese
green salad ingredients
50 g/2 oz walnut halves

Blend all the ingredients for the dressing in a good-sized bowl. Peel and slice the pears, cut the cheese into 4 portions. Leave both pears and cheese in the dressing until ready to serve. Arrange the salad ingredients on 4 plates, place the cheese in the centre, with the pear slices and walnuts around the cheese, top with the dressing.

To make a change
Halve and core the peeled pears, fill with cream cheese blended with chopped walnuts and sour cream. Use the dressing and salad as above.
  You can also use avocados in place of dessert pears.

Globe Artichokes with Fish Pâté

Choose firm artichokes and use as soon as possible after purchase. Stand the stalks in water until you are ready to cook. The pâté should be made a little softer than usual. Eat by pulling away individual leaves and dipping the tender base in the pâté. Discard the harder tips. Finger bowls are essential when serving this hors d'oeuvre and remember to provide a plate for the debris.

> 4 to 6 globe artichokes
> salt and freshly ground black pepper
> 1 lemon slice
> *For the pâté*:
> 100 g/4 oz cooked salmon or white fish, such as
>   sole or turbot
> 100 g/4 oz smoked salmon, trout* or mackerel*
> 1 garlic clove, optional
> 50 g/2 oz butter
> 1 tablespoon lemon juice
> 3 to 4 tablespoons double cream or thick
>   yoghurt
> 1 teaspoon chopped fennel leaves
> *To garnish*:
> lettuce leaves and lemon wedges

Wash the artichokes. The centre chokes can be cut out before, or after, cooking. Put into boiling, seasoned water with the lemon slice. Artichokes keep a better colour if cooked in an enamel saucepan. Cook steadily for 25 to 40 minutes – the time varies according to the size and maturity of the vegetables. When cooked a single leaf comes away easily and is soft at the base. Drain and remove the centre choke if not done already. Trim the base so the artichokes stand steadily. Allow to become quite cold.

Dice the fish, peel and crush the garlic. Melt the butter. Pound the fish, butter and garlic or put into a food processor and switch on for a few seconds. Add the lemon juice, seasoning and cream or yoghurt to make a soft pâté. Add the fennel and any extra seasoning desired. Arrange the artichokes on the lettuce, spoon the pâté in the centre and garnish with the lemon wedges. **Serves 4 to 6**

* Use a little horseradish cream in the pâté with either of these.

Duck with Apple Coulis

The term coulis is used a good deal these days. It describes a clear and not too thick, refreshing savoury, or sweet sauce – made without flour thickening. Although the duck, or quail, can be served cold, these are far nicer as a hot contrast to the crisp cold salad.

For the coulis:
300 ml/½ pint thick lightly sweetened apple
 purée
2 tablespoons apple or redcurrant or cranberry
 jelly
2 tablespoons Calvados

1 duckling or 4 duck portions, cooked as p.135
For the salad:
crisp lettuce of various kinds
4 to 6 tablespoons diced red pepper
oil and vinegar dressing, *see* **page 146**

Heat the apple purée with the jelly, sieve or liquidize if necessary, add the Calvados and chill. Cut the cooked duck into narrow ribbons. The crisp skin can be left on, in which case make sure it is uppermost when serving the dish. Arrange the salad and coulis on individual plates. Top with a little dressing just before serving, then add the hot duck.   *Serves 4 to 6*

To make a change
Use halved grapes instead of red pepper in the salad above.
Spiced Quail: Try to buy boned quail. Allow one per person. For 4 to 6 quail make a marinade of 150 ml/¼ pint red wine, 2 tablespoons olive oil, 1 peeled and crushed garlic clove, 1 teaspoon Juniper berries plus ½ teaspoon ground cinnamon and a good shake of freshly ground black pepper. Leave the birds in this for 3 to 4 hours. Drain and roast as the instructions on page 146. Make the coulis with the apples, plus the jelly, as in the recipe above, but add 2 tablespoons of the strained marinade instead of the Calvados.
Smoked Turkey or Chicken: Serve cold with salad. Make a coulis with 225 g /8 oz sieved, cooked, sweetened cranberries, the jelly and red wine or port.

Game Pâté

Most game birds make a good pâté, for they have a definite taste. The recipe below uses pheasant, which has plenty of flesh on the bones, but you can use a good-sized grouse or 2 to 3 partridge instead.

> 1 young pheasant
> 175 g/6 oz fat bacon
> 100 g/4 oz calves' or lambs' liver
> liver from the pheasant
> 1 large green pepper
> 1 egg
> 3 tablespoons brandy or pheasant stock, *see* *
> pinch allspice
> ½ teaspoon chopped thyme or ¼ teaspoon
>   dried thyme
> salt and freshly ground black pepper
> *For lining the dish:*
> 225 g/8 oz long streaky bacon rashers

Preheat the oven to 150°C/300°F, Gas Mark 2. Cut the breast from the pheasant, remove the skin and slice the flesh; cover and put on one side. Cut away all the flesh from the rest of the bird. Dice the bacon and liver. Put the pheasant meat, bacon and liver through a fine mincer, or into a food processor. Do not *over*-process or the texture will be sticky.

Halve the pepper and remove the core and seeds. Put under a preheated grill for 2 to 3 minutes or until the skin darkens. Remove the skin. Dice the pepper finely. Blend with the pheasant pâté, then add the egg, brandy or pheasant stock* – made by simmering the carcass of the bird in water to cover. Stir in the allspice, thyme and seasoning.

Derind the bacon rashers. Line a 900 g/2 lb ovenproof dish with these, making sure there is enough length to cover the mixture. Put half the pheasant mixture into the bacon-lined dish, add the sliced breast meat, then the rest of the minced pheasant. Fold the bacon rashers over this mixture. Add a lid or foil covering.

Stand in a tin half-filled with cold water. Cook for 2 hours. Remove the lid and cover the pâté with a piece of foil and a light weight. Leave until cold, remove any surplus fat from the pâté. Turn out and slice. Serve with hot toast and butter and cranberry or redcurrant jelly.   *Serves 4 to 6*

Rillettes

Rillettes are true country fare and although they vary slightly in different regions of France, basically they are made by cooking a mixture of lean and fat pork for a long time in lard, with various herbs and seasonings. Sometimes a small amount of goose is cooked with the pork. The mixture is then pounded until almost as smooth as a pâté. I have borrowed the name to describe an economical mixture made from the giblets of birds such as turkey, duck, goose or chicken.

Most of us simmer the giblets to make stock for sauce or gravy to serve with roast poultry, and this makes very good use of all the giblet meat.

> cooked giblets from 1 large turkey or goose or
>   2 ducks or 2 medium chickens
> 2 small onions
> 1 to 2 garlic cloves
> 100 g/4 oz streaky bacon rashers
> 25 g/1 oz butter or 1 tablespoon sunflower oil
>   *or* fat from cooking the bird(s)
> 1 teaspoon chopped rosemary or ½ teaspoon
>   dried rosemary
> salt and freshly ground black pepper
> 1 teaspoon Dijon mustard
> 1 to 2 tablespoons sherry or giblet stock

Take all the meat from the giblets. Peel and finely chop the onions, garlic and bacon rashers; save the bacon rinds. Heat these with the butter or oil or fat and cook the onion, garlic and bacon until just tender. Mix with the giblet meat and either pound or mince or put into the food processor until a smooth mixture. Blend with the rosemary, seasonings and sherry or stock to give the required consistency. Cover and allow to cool. Serve as pâté, *see* page 92, or for a main meal with a mixed salad.

To make a change
To give a more traditional flavour, mince or process 175 g/6 oz cooked pork with the other ingredients. If the pork is lean use double the amount of fat or oil given in the recipe above when cooking the onions and garlic.

It is possible to make a similar mixture with small pieces of cooked poultry flesh in addition to the giblets.

Escargots in a Nest

The recipes on this page are based on a well-flavoured butter.

For the garlic butter:
2 to 3 garlic cloves, or to taste
100 g/4 oz butter
salt and freshly ground black pepper

1 large or 2 small French loaves
approximately 24 fresh or canned snails

Preheat the oven to 200°C/400°F, Gas Mark 6. Peel and crush the garlic, add to the butter with a little seasoning.

Cut 12 slices of bread. Scoop out a cavity in the centre of each slice without going right through. Spread the slices with half the garlic butter. Put on baking trays. Heat for 6 to 7 minutes. Put 2 snails in each cavity. Top with the remaining garlic butter. Bake for a further 5 minutes.

Fried Stuffed Avocados

For the herb butter:
75 g/3 oz butter
1 tablespoon lemon juice
2 tablespoons chopped mixed herbs
salt and freshly ground black pepper

4 ripe avocados
1 egg white
4 tablespoons fine crisp breadcrumbs
oil for frying

Blend the ingredients for the herb butter. Peel, halve and stone the avocados. Fill the holes with the butter. Join the halves together with wooden toothpicks. Coat in the egg white and crumbs. Deep fry in hot oil for 3 to 4 minutes; drain well. Remove toothpicks and serve at once.

SOUPS

As a lover of soup I found it very difficult to choose just a few for this book. I make soups, to serve either hot or cold, with great regularity and I use a wide range of recipes. In the end I have selected those that have something rather special to offer.

Oatmeal Soup and the very satisfying Bortsch on p.96 – not unlike an American thick chowder – serve as reminders of the war years. That does not mean they are ultra-economical and dull; on the contrary, with the additional ingredients we can incorporate today they are interesting and very tasty.

Oatmeal Soup

This recipe uses quick-cooking rolled oats, rather than the old-fashioned oatmeal that took longer to cook. Oatmeal in any form adds essential fibre to the diet, so here you have a soup of high nutritional value as well as one with a good flavour.

This soup can be cooked in the microwave. Use a large, uncovered bowl and the same quantity of liquid. Follow the timing recommended for porridge after cooking the vegetables.

> **2 medium onions**
> **2 to 3 medium carrots**
> **½ green pepper**
> **½ red pepper**
> **25 g/1 oz butter or margarine**
> **600 ml/1 pint chicken stock or water**
> **25 g/1 oz rolled (porridge) oats**
> **salt and freshly ground black pepper**
> **150 ml/¼ pint milk**
> **150 ml/¼ pint single cream**
> *To garnish:*
> **chopped chives**

Peel and finely chop the onions. Peel and finely grate the carrots. Dice the peppers very finely. Heat the butter or margarine and toss the vegetables in this for 2 or 3 minutes. Then add the stock or water together with the rolled oats. Stir well as the liquid comes to the boil.

Add seasoning to taste. Cover the pan and simmer gently for 10 minutes, then add the milk and cream and heat. Top with the chives.

Bortsch

This soup was popular during the years of rationing. In those days the soup was made with water; but beef stock, or stock from boiling bacon, gives a much richer flavour. The soured cream topping would *not* have appeared in those far-off days and in wintertime you would have omitted the tomatoes, unless you had some stored in bottling jars.

1 large or 2 medium raw beetroot
2 medium potatoes
2 medium carrots
2 medium onions
1 small parsnip
3 large tomatoes
½ small cabbage
25 g/1 oz beef or bacon fat or margarine
1.2 litres/2 pints beef or bacon stock or water
  (more may be required, *see* method)
salt and freshly ground black pepper
4 fresh or 2 dried bay leaves, or to taste
To garnish:
chopped parsley
soured cream

Peel and grate the beetroot, potatoes, carrots, onions and parsnip. Concass the tomatoes – this means skinning them, removing all the seeds then chopping the pulp. Shred the cabbage finely. Heat the fat or margarine and toss the vegetables, except the tomatoes and cabbage, in this for 2 or 3 minutes. Add the stock and bring to the boil.

Put in the tomatoes, cabbage, a little seasoning and the bay leaves. Cover the pan tightly and simmer gently for 1½ to 2 hours. Check the amount of liquid during this time and add more if required.

Remove the bay leaves and serve the soup topped with parsley and a generous amount of soured cream.

To make a change
Speedy Bortsch: Use 2 large cooked beetroot. Grate the other vegetables finely, toss in the fat, add the stock, tomatoes and cabbage. Cook for 30 minutes Add the peeled and grated beetroot and heat for 10 minutes.

Seafood Bisque

The recipe can be adapted for use with any fish you have available, although traditionally it is made with fish which colours the dish pink.

175 g/6 oz prawns in their shells
1 small cooked lobster, preferably a hen
1 shallot or small onion
50 g/2 oz butter
50 g/2 oz flour
900 ml/1½ pints milk
salt and cayenne pepper
3 tablespoons double cream

Remove the prawns and lobster from their shells; put the coral (roe) to one side. Wash the shells and put in a pan with water to cover. Simmer for 15 minutes, until 150 ml/¼ pint liquid remains. This stock gives colour and flavour to the soup. Chop the seafood finely.

Peel and chop the shallot or onion finely, melt the butter, cook the shallot or onion until soft, stir in the flour, then gradually blend in the milk and stock. Stir as the sauce comes to the boil and thickens, then add the seasoning, the seafood, including the coral, and the cream. Heat gently for a few minutes.   *Serves 4 to 6*

Cream of Chicken Soup

The success of this soup depends entirely on using a good chicken stock. It's worth keeping keeping a supply in your freezer.

Ingredients as in the soup above but omit the
seafood and use 225 g/8 oz cooked chicken
breast with 450 ml/¾ pint strongly flavoured
chicken stock and 600 ml/1 pint milk.

Chop the chicken. Cook the shallot or onion in the butter as above. Add the flour, milk, stock and seasoning. Bring to the boil. When thickened, add the chicken then sieve or liquidize. Return to the pan with the cream. Heat gently.

Czech Potato Soup

These soups are entirely different. One is a hot and satisfying family soup; the second a classic cold dish. But both depend upon the humble potato, which should not be neglected. It is a delicious vegetable with a high vitamin content.

2 medium onions
4 medium potatoes
2 celery sticks
1 red pepper
50 g/2 oz butter or margarine
900 ml/1½ pints water
salt and freshly ground black pepper
150 ml/¼ pint milk
To garnish:
little soured cream
paprika

Peel the onions and potatoes. Chop the celery and onions, finely dice the potatoes and deseeded pepper. Heat the butter or margarine, add the vegetables and cook for 5 minutes, then pour in the water. Bring to the boil and then add the seasoning. Cover the pan; cook steadily for 20 minutes, or until the vegetables are tender. Add the milk, heat gently then serve topped with soured cream and a good shake of paprika.

Vichysoisse

6 medium leeks
2 medium potatoes
50 g/2 oz butter
600 ml/1 pint chicken stock
1 tablespoon chopped parsley
1 tablespoon chopped chives
salt and freshly ground black pepper
300 ml/½ pint single cream
150 ml/¼ pint dry white wine
To garnish:
little finely chopped parsley
little finely chopped chives

Clean the leeks, remove all the tough green part* but leave just a little green stem, for this helps to give a good colour to the soup, then slice the leeks. Peel and dice the potatoes. Heat the butter and toss the vegetables in this for 5 minutes. Add the stock, herbs and a little seasoning. Bring to the boil, cover the pan and cook for 15 to 20 minutes. Sieve or liquidize the mixture. Cool, then blend in the cream and wine with any extra seasoning required. Serve very cold, topped with herbs.   *Serves 4 to 6*

* Vegetarians may like to use the green tops as the basis for a leek stock, to use in place of the chicken stock in the recipe.

Gazpacho

Do not use canned or cooked tomatoes for this dish.

> **675 g/1½ lb ripe tomatoes**
> **1 small cucumber**
> **2 garlic cloves**
> **2 large onions or equivalent in spring onions or**
> **shallots**
> **1 green pepper**
> **1 red pepper**
> **2 to 3 tablespoons olive oil, or to taste**
> **salt and freshly ground black pepper**
> **lemon juice or white wine vinegar**
> **iced water**
> **several slices of bread**

Chop the tomatoes, peel the cucumber and cut into small, neat dice. Peel and finely chop the garlic and onions or shallots; deseed and dice the peppers.

Put half the cucumber, onions and peppers into small dishes to serve with the soup. Liquidize or, better still, sieve the tomatoes, remaining cucumber, onions, peppers and garlic, to give a smooth mixture. Add olive oil, seasoning and lemon juice or vinegar to taste and enough iced water to give a flowing consistency.

Chill the soup very well. Remove the crusts from the bread and cut the rest into small dice. Put into a dish. Serve the soup with the dishes of cucumber, onions, peppers and bread. Each person helps themselves to this garnish.   *Serves 4 to 6*

Iced Avocado and Lemon Soup

I have suggested chicken stock for this soup and for Iced Cucumber Soup, but vegetarians could equally well use vegetable stock.

2 large ripe avocados
2 tablespoons lemon juice
300 ml/½ pint yoghurt
450 ml/¾ pint chicken stock
salt and freshly ground black pepper

Skin the avocados, halve and remove the stones. Liquidize with the lemon juice, yoghurt and stock, season to taste and chill well.

Iced Cucumber Soup

1 medium cucumber
2 tablespoons mint leaves, or to taste
300 ml/½ pint single cream or fromage frais
1 tablespoon lemon juice or white wine vinegar
450 ml/¾ pint chicken stock
salt and freshly ground black pepper

Peel the cucumber and cut into slices. Save a few mint leaves and a little cream or fromage frais to garnish the soup. Liquidize all the rest of the ingredients. Put into the freezer for a short time, until lightly frosted, then spoon into soup cups. Garnish and serve.

Iced Fruit Soups

Make thick, and lightly sweetened, purées from sharp fruits like apples, rhubarb or cooking plums, or with cooked dried fruits. Blend with dry white wine or with cider. Freeze lightly and serve topped with yoghurt or fromage frais.

FISH DISHES

The huge variety of fish available today means we can create fish dishes with many exciting tastes and textures. Some of the recipes that follow are made with a specific fish, if this is not available, or not good on a particular day, choose one that is of the same variety; e.g. another oily fish, such as fresh mackerel or trout, instead of herrings; or a fine-textured white fish in place of sole.

Be very critical when buying fish. Make sure it is really fresh: there should be no smell of ammonia. That means the fish is stale.

Fish with Dates

This Moroccan dish is delicious. Fresh dates are definitely best, but you can substitute dessert-type dates (not the cooking variety).

> 1 kg/2¼ lb haddock or codling, weight when
>   boned
> salt and freshly ground black pepper
> *For the stuffing:*
> 50 g/2 oz butter or margarine
> 150 g/5 oz cooked rice
> 225 g/8 oz fresh dates, weight when stoned
> 1 teaspoon sugar
> 50 g/2 oz blanched almonds
> pinch ground ginger
> pinch ground cinnamon
> *To cook the fish:*
> 1 large onion
> 150 ml/¼ pint water

Cut open the fish and season it. Melt the butter or margarine and mix with the stuffing ingredients. Put into the fish; secure with a fine skewer.

Peel and thinly slice the onion, put into a casserole with the water and a little seasoning. Add the fish, cover the dish. Cook for 30 to 40 minutes in a preheated oven, set to 190°C/375°F, Gas Mark 5.

To make a change
Dried prunes or apricots can be used instead of dates. Lightly cook, then drain these, unless using the tenderized varieties.

Fish in Sesame and Ginger

Both recipes on this page are for dishes that can be made in minutes. Use a wok in the first recipe if possible – this gives quicker heating – and choose a firm-fleshed fish, some varieties are suggested in the recipe.

Bone fresh sardines for the second dish.

> 450 g/1 lb cod or salmon or tuna, weight
>   without skin and bones
> 1 egg white
> 2 teaspoons cornflour
> salt and freshly ground black pepper
> 2 teaspoons sesame seeds
> 3 shallots or 1 medium onion
> 1 green pepper
> 1 red pepper
> 1 tablespoon sesame oil
> 1 tablespoon sunflower oil
> 1 tablespoon grated fresh ginger
> 1 to 2 tablespoons light soy sauce
> 150 ml/¼ pint rice wine or white wine

Cut the fish into 2.5 cm/1 inch cubes. Brush with egg white. Mix the cornflour, seasoning and sesame seeds and coat the fish with this. Peel and finely chop the shallots or onion; deseed and dice the peppers. Heat the oils (do not exceed the amount of sesame oil stated above). Put in the fish and stir-fry until just golden. Remove from the pan. Add the shallots or onion; stir-fry for several minutes, then add the peppers and cook for another minute. Put in the ginger, soy sauce and wine and heat for a minute before adding the fish. Continue stir-frying for 3 to 4 minutes.

Serve with cooked rice and peas.

Fresh Sardines

There are many ways of cooking these delicious small fish. One of the nicest is under a preheated grill (broiler) or over a barbecue.

Season the fish, flavour with a little lemon juice and chopped mixed herbs. Grill or barbecue for 5 to 6 minutes, turning over once.

Crab Gumbo

This Creole-inspired dish is often served as a soup but it is so satisfying that I prefer it as a main course with a crisp green salad. The essential ingredient, that provides the sticky texture, is the okra, a vegetable also known as ladies' fingers. This is obtainable fresh, but the canned variety could be used instead.

> **350 g/12 oz okra**
> **salt and freshly ground black pepper**
> **1 medium onion**
> **1 garlic clove**
> **1 green pepper**
> **1 lemon**
> **675 g/1½ lb plum tomatoes or use a can of**
> **chopped tomatoes**
> **2 tablespoons olive oil**
> **450 g/1 lb crabmeat**
> **150 ml/¼ pint double cream**

Try and buy small okra, so they can be cooked whole. If large cut into slices. Put into boiling, seasoned water and cook for 5 to 6 minutes, until just tender, then strain. Peel and finely chop the onion and garlic, deseed and dice the pepper. Pare the top zest from the lemon, squeeze out the juice. Skin and chop the tomatoes.

Heat the oil in a pan and add the onion and garlic. Cook for 5 minutes. Put in the tomatoes (use the liquid from the can) plus the pepper and lemon zest. Season lightly, then cover the pan and simmer for 10 minutes or until the onion is tender. Remove the lemon zest. Add the crabmeat, okra and lemon juice to taste and then heat thoroughly. Remove from the heat then stir in the cream and seasoning to taste. Heat gently, without boiling (boiling will cause the mixture to curdle). Serve with hot, crusty bread.

To make a change
Use peeled prawns or flaked lobster or even diced fish instead (diced white fish, tuna or salmon are all suitable). If using uncooked fish, simmer for a short time in the tomato mixture.

This dish can be given a hotter flavour by including a good pinch of chilli powder or a few drops of Tabasco sauce.

Cioppino

This dish is a wonderful mixture of flavours. It is a dish to serve when you are entertaining; for it is not exactly cheap. The fish stock is an important ingredient.

1 medium lobster
350 g/12 oz prawns in their shells
1.2 litres/2 pints mussels
2 medium onions
2 garlic cloves
150 ml/¼ pint fish stock, *see* method
1 green pepper
450 g/1 lb fish – sea-bass is an ideal choice
350 g/12 oz tomatoes
2 tablespoons olive oil
1 to 2 tablespoons tomato purée (paste)
150 ml/¼ pint white wine
salt and freshly ground black pepper
To garnish:
chopped parsley

Remove the lobster and prawns from the shells. Keep the shells. Scrub the mussels, discard any that are open and do not close when tapped sharply. Peel and finely chop the onions and garlic. Put the mussels, with half the onion into a good-sized saucepan, add water to cover. Heat steadily for a few minutes, or until the mussels open. Discard any that remain closed. Save the liquid. Add the lobster and prawn shells to the liquid and simmer for 10 minutes. Strain and retain 150 ml/¼ pint.

Deseed and dice the pepper. Cut the sea-bass, or other fish, into small neat pieces. Skin, deseed and chop the tomatoes. Heat the oil in a large saucepan, add the remaining onion and the garlic. Cook steadily for 3 or 4 minutes. Add the chopped tomatoes, tomato purée, fish stock and white wine. Stir well to blend. Cover the pan and simmer for 10 minutes then add the diced fish and cook for 5 to 8 minutes, or until almost tender.

Dice the lobster. The mussels can be removed from both shells, or they can be kept on a single shell. Add all the shellfish to the other ingredients and heat thoroughly; do *not* overcook, as that will toughen the fish. Season to taste. Top with chopped parsley. **Serves 4 to 6**

Gulai Ikan

This Indonesian fish dish is at its best when made with fresh tuna but you can use any firm textured fish instead. Suggestions are given in the list of ingredients.

> 450 to 550 g/1 to 1¼ lb fresh tuna or use large
>   fresh mackerel or shark
> salt and freshly ground black pepper
> 2 medium onions
> 2 garlic cloves
> 300 ml/½ pint coconut milk, *see* method
> 2 teaspoons grated ginger
> ½ teaspoon turmeric
> good pinch chilli powder
> 1 lemon grass stalk or use 2 or 3 teaspoons of
>   grated lemon zest
> 150 ml/¼ pint tamarind* purée or use fresh
>   tomato purée if this is not available

Cut the fish into neat pieces; you will need a rather greater weight of mackerel, because of the high percentage of head, skin and bone. Season the fish well. Peel and finely chop the onions and garlic.

To make the coconut milk: There are various ways of preparing this. The simplest and best for this recipe is to pour 300 ml/½ pint boiling water over 50 g/2 oz desiccated coconut. Leave until cold then put into a liquidizer to make a smooth liquid. You can also heat 75 g/3 oz creamed coconut in 300 ml/½ pint water until dissolved and use this.

Put the onion and garlic into a saucepan, add half the coconut milk, the ginger, turmeric and chilli powder. Chop the lemon grass and add this, or use the lemon zest. Cover the pan and cook gently for 10 minutes, or until the onion and garlic are tender. Add the tamarind or tomato purée and the fish and cook steadily for 10 to 15 minutes in the covered pan, until the fish is tender. Do not allow the mixture to boil. Stir in the rest of the coconut milk and extra seasoning just before the end of the cooking time. Serve with rice.

* This fruit is used widely in Indonesia as a flavouring. It has an acid taste. The juice is added to some curries. You may have to use canned fruit to obtain a purée. If substituting tomato purée, be generous with the lemon flavouring.

Scampi Spumante

Scampi are the large version of prawns caught in the Adriatic; there are many alternatives. You can use the tails of langoustines or Dublin Bay prawns or even large ordinary prawns or shrimps. If using frozen scampi, allow to defrost thoroughly before using in either of these recipes.

> **about 24 shelled scampi or equivalent in frozen**
> **scampi or smaller shellfish**
> **1 shallot or small onion**
> **225 g/8 oz button mushrooms**
> **25 g/1 oz butter**
> **1 tablespoon olive oil**
> **150 ml/¼ pint white wine,** *see* **method**
> **2 egg yolks**
> **150 ml/¼ pint double cream**
> **salt and freshly ground black pepper**

Dry the shellfish well on kitchen paper. Peel and finely chop the shallot or onion. Wipe and slice the mushrooms. Heat the butter. Add the shallot or onion and cook gently for 3 minutes, taking care that it does not brown. Stir in the mushrooms and fish and continue cooking for 2 minutes. Add the wine; heat for 4 to 7 minutes depending upon the size of the fish. Remove the pan from the heat.

Whisk the egg yolks and cream and add 2 tablespoons of the hot wine. Beat well, then tip into the pan and stir over a very, very low heat, until it makes a thick, creamy sauce. Serve at once with cooked rice or pasta.

Scampi Capriccio

> **scampi or alternative fish, as above**
> **Mornay Sauce,** *see* **page 143**
> **dry sherry to taste**
> **chopped parsley**

Dry the scampi well. Put into the sauce and heat gently until completely cooked. Remove from the heat, whisk in the sherry and reheat, without boiling. Add the parsley. Serve with cooked rice or pasta.

Shrimps in Lime and Coconut Sauce

This dish can be made with large prawns or with tiny shrimps. If using frozen shellfish, defrost and dry very well on kitchen paper before heating. A wok is an ideal cooking utensil for this dish.

1 large or 2 small limes
450 g/1 lb peeled prawns or shrimps
300 ml/½ pint coconut milk, *see* page 105
1 tablespoon sunflower oil
2 teaspoons light soy sauce
salt and freshly ground black pepper
To garnish:
little chopped lemon grass or parsley

Grate the top zest from the limes and squeeze out enough juice to give 2 tablespoons, or a little more if preferred. Blend the fish with the lime zest. Cover and leave in the refrigerator for an hour, so the lime flavour penetrates the shellfish.

Make the coconut milk, as on page 105. Heat the oil, toss the shellfish in it for 1 or 2 minutes, then add the coconut milk, soy sauce and lime juice. Season to taste and heat thoroughly, but do not allow to boil.

Top with the lemon grass or parsley and serve with cooked rice.

Oyster Sauce

This delicious sauce transforms chicken, or white fish, into a truly memorable dish.

8 large or 12 small oysters
50 g/2 oz button mushrooms
50 g/2 oz butter
150 ml/¼ pint single cream
salt and freshly ground white pepper

Lift the oysters from their shells. Save any juice. Chop finely. Wipe and slice the mushrooms. Heat the butter. Toss the mushrooms in this then add the oysters, juice, cream and seasoning and heat for a few minutes.

Devilled Herrings

It has been said that if herrings were an expensive fish we would appreciate them more. Few fish have a better taste or are as adaptable. From herrings we obtain soft and hard roes, smoked kippers, bloaters or buckling. The latter was once a great favourite in Britain but is seen less frequently these days. Rollmops and all forms of pickled herring, make excellent hors d'oeuvre. If you are a herring lover you should visit Scandinavia, where the fish is served in many ways. Choose plump fish that feel heavy for their size.

> **4 large herrings, with soft roes**
> *For the filling and topping*:
> **75 g/3 oz butter or margarine**
> **1 to 2 teaspoons curry paste or powder**
> **3 tablespoons finely chopped spring onions or**
>   **shallots**
> **1 teaspoon Worcestershire sauce**
> **1 to 2 teaspoons made English mustard**
> **salt and cayenne pepper**

To bone the fish: Remove the heads and split the herrings down the underside, remove the roes and put on one side. Discard the other intestines. Open the fish out flat, lay on a board with the cut side downwards; run your forefinger down the centre of the fish, turn over and you can then remove the backbone and other bones.

Cream the butter or margarine and blend with the other ingredients. Spread a little of the mixture over the opened fish, add the roes then fold the fish, to enclose the roes. Place on an ovenproof serving dish. Top with the rest of the mixture. Do not cover the dish. Bake for 25 minutes in a preheated oven set to 190°C/375°F, Gas Mark 5.

Serve with a salad and creamed or new potatoes or cooked rice.

Crunchy Herrings

Bone the herrings, as above; leave the fish flat. Coat the herrings and the roes in beaten egg then in fine oatmeal, or rolled (porridge) oats. Fry in a little hot fat or oil until crisp and brown. Serve with lemon.

Sole Normandy

There are many classic recipes featuring sole, but this one, which includes mussels, is one of my favourites.

If you are not a mussel lover, you can use peeled prawns instead

> 600 ml/1 pint mussels
> 1 small onion
> 1 sprig of parsley
> 8 sole fillets, preferably skinned
> salt and freshly ground white pepper
> *For the wine sauce:*
> 600 ml/1 pint white wine
> 40 g/1½ oz butter
> 40 g/1½ oz plain flour

Scrub the mussels, discarding any that do not close. Peel and chop the onion and put the mussels, onion and parsley into a saucepan. Cover with water and heat until opened (*see* page 104). Remove from the shells. Return to the liquid until ready to use.

Lay the sole fillets flat in a lightly buttered casserole, or fold each fillet in half. Add a little seasoning and the wine. Cover the fish with buttered greaseproof paper. Bake for 20 minutes, or until just cooked, in a preheated oven, set to 200°C/400°F, Gas Mark 6. Lift the sole carefully on to a heated serving dish, cover and keep hot.

Heat the butter in a pan. Stir in the flour. Strain the liquid from the casserole into the pan, then whisk as the sauce comes to the boil and thickens. If it is a little too thick, add more wine or use a little of the strained liquid in which the mussels were opened. Season to taste. Pour over and around the fish. Garnish with the mussels.

To make a change
Instead of using all wine, simmer the skins and bones of the sole in water to cover to make stock, blend with the mussel liquid and use this to make the sauce instead of some of the white wine.

To grill sole: Sole is also delicious simply grilled. The secret of beautifully moist grilled sole, or other white fish, is to marinate it in milk for an hour, then drain it well before brushing with melted butter and cooking.

Salmon in a Crust

When I was young, this dish was a great treat and I still enjoy food wrapped in a delicate pastry crust, or *en croute* as it is now called. In those days frozen puff pastry was a thing of the future. I have used frozen pastry here to make the dish easier.

> 1 kg/2½ lb piece of salmon
> salt and freshly ground black pepper
> little lemon juice
> 1 sprig of parsley
> *For the stuffing:*
> 1 medium onion
> 225 g/8 oz flat mushrooms
> 40 g/1½ oz butter
> 2 tablespoons chopped parsley
> 1 teaspoon chopped dill or fennel leaves
>
> 225 g/8 oz frozen puff pastry
> 1 egg

Put the salmon into a pan with water to cover. Add seasoning, lemon juice and parsley. Bring to simmering point and cook gently for 20 minutes, or until the salmon is lightly cooked. Remove from the liquid, cover and allow to cool, then remove skin and bones without damaging the shape of the fish. Peel and finely chop the onion; wipe and chop the mushrooms. Heat the butter and cook the onion until tender. Add the mushrooms, but do not cook; mix with the herbs and seasoning. Leave until quite cold. Allow the pastry to defrost, then roll out thinly.

Roll to an oblong shape large enough to envelop the fish. Trim to the size desired. Spread with the stuffing, keeping it away from the edges. Place the fish in the centre of the pastry. Moisten the edges, fold the pastry over the fish, seal and flute the edges then turn over, so the join is underneath. Make slits in the pastry and brush this with beaten egg. Any pastry left can be made into leaves and placed on top of the pastry. Put on a baking tray; chill for a time before cooking.

Bake for 35 minutes in a preheated oven, set to 220°C/425°F, Gas Mark 7. Lower heat after 20 minutes if pastry is becoming too brown. Serve with a creamy white sauce, flavoured with fennel or dill.   *Serves 6*

Itsy-Bitsy Salmon

This is really a salmon kedgeree, but Itsy-Bitsy Salmon was the ridiculous name by which I knew this delicious dish when I was a child, because of the small portions of cooked salmon which lurked in it. My aunt, who concocted it, was certainly an inventive cook. Over the years I have created my own recipes for using a small amount of salmon. Some of them are on this page.

>225 g/8 oz cooked salmon
>1 medium onion
>¼ small cucumber
>40 g/1½ oz butter or margarine
>225 g/8 oz cooked long grain rice
>150 ml/¼ pint single cream or milk
>2 hard-boiled eggs
>few cooked peas

Cut the salmon into neat pieces but do not flake too finely. Peel and finely chop the onion; peel and finely dice the cucumber. Heat the butter or margarine in a saucepan, add the onion and cook gently until soft, then put in the cucumber and rice and turn in the onion mixture. Add the salmon with the cream or milk. Heat the ingredients gently, stirring as little as possible so that the fish is left unbroken.

Chop the egg whites and yolks separately. Stir the whites into the salmon mixture with the peas. Heat for 1 or 2 minutes. Spoon into a pyramid shape and top with the chopped hard-boiled egg yolks.

To make a change
Kedgeree Salad: Use finely chopped spring onions instead of an ordinary onion and omit the butter. Blend the cooked salmon, rice and peas with raw cucumber, raw onions, mayonnaise and cream to make a soft consistency. Top with chopped hard-boiled egg whites and yolks.
Potted Salmon: Blend the flaked cooked salmon with 50 g/2 oz melted butter, 2 teaspoons chopped fennel leaves, 1 tablespoon dry sherry, 2 tablespoons pine kernels and a little salt and cayenne pepper. Spoon into a container, cover and chill. Serve as a pâté.
Salmon Fish Cakes: Blend equal amounts of flaked, cooked salmon with mashed potatoes. Bind with an egg and form into cakes. Coat with beaten egg and crisp breadcrumbs. Fry until crisp and brown.

MEAT – POULTRY – GAME

In Britain we have a wonderful tradition of fine quality meats and although most of the dishes that follow come from other countries, I always feel our produce enhances their flavour. The fact that I have selected many recipes that come from abroad does not mean I do not enjoy, or appreciate, our own traditional cooking. I think British food at its best is some of the finest in the world, but in this particular book I have selected recipes that are bound up with my various travels and experiences and which I have found particularly good.

The recipe that follows comes from Morocco. It demands fine quality meat.

Kababs

This looks as if I have spelt kebabs incorrectly, but in fact kababs is the correct Arabic spelling and the one used in Morocco to describe cubes of meat cooked on skewers. It is a dish that typifies some Arab cooking, which can be very simple. If you can use best quality mutton, rather than lamb, you will have the true flavour of the dish.

> **450 g/1 lb mutton or lamb or beef fillet**
> **225 g/8 oz fat meat,** *see* **method***
> **2 medium onions**
> **2 tablespoons finely chopped parsley**
> **good pinch ground cumin**
> **good pinch cayenne pepper**
> **very little salt**

Cut the meat into 3.5 cm/1½ inch cubes. Cut the fat meat into cubes of about half that size. *As today's meats are so lean you may have to buy a little fat pork instead, or use fat bacon. Peel and grate or mince or chop the onions so they are very fine. Put the meats with the onions and any onion juice that comes from mincing them, plus the parsley, spices and salt into a bowl, turn around and leave for several hours, so all the flavours blend. Thread on to metal skewers. Alternate between lean and fat meat. Grill or barbecue for several minutes. Turn once or twice so the meat is evenly cooked. Serve with cooked rice and salad, or with couscous.

Corned Beef Hash

During the years of rationing we ate a great deal of corned beef, got very tired of the flavour and exhausted all inspired ideas for cooking it. It went right out of fashion. When I was in New York in the sixties, however, I watched people tucking into Corned Beef Hash and ordered some for myself. It not only brought back memories of wartime but also reminded me that this particular dish was very pleasant. Since that time, I serve it at home from time to time and we thoroughly enjoy it.

If you have any leftover cooked salted silverside or brisket of beef you could use that instead of the canned corned beef. Mince or finely chop these meats to give the right texture.

> **1 medium onion**
> **50 g/2 oz butter**
> **350 g/12 oz corned beef**
> **225 g/8 oz cooked potatoes**
> **4 tablespoons single cream or milk or beef stock**
> **salt and freshly ground black pepper**

Peel and chop the onion. Heat half the butter in a large frying pan, add the onion and cook for several minutes. Tip into a large bowl, add the beef and potatoes and mash together until a smooth mixture. Gradually add the liquid (cream gives a splendid taste) and seasoning.

Heat the remaining butter, put in the mixture and spread evenly over the pan. Cook gently for about 30 minutes, scraping the base from time to time to blend in the brown bits. Fold like an omelette and serve. Cooked beetroot or pickled red cabbage make excellent accompaniments.

To make a change

Add finely chopped red and/or green peppers or 2 tablespoons chopped parsley to the mixture before cooking.

Baked Hash: Choose an ovenproof serving dish, as it is difficult to turn out this version of the hash. Spread the mixture into the buttered dish and bake for 30 minutes in a preheated oven, set to 190°C/375°F, Gas Mark 5.

Corned Beef Fritters: Make a thick batter with 100 g/4 oz self-raising flour, pinch of salt, 1 egg and 150 ml/¼ pint milk. Flake 225 g/8 oz corned beef, add to the batter with 2 tablespoons of chopped parsley and the same amount of chopped spring onions or chives. Fry spoonfuls of the mixture in hot oil or fat until crisp and brown. Drain and serve.

113

Hamburgers

Although an American speciality, the original home of these meat cakes, as the name suggests, was Hamburg in Germany. Nowadays hamburgers, served in buns, have become a popular dish all over the world. Their flavour varies with the quality of the meat. For prime hamburgers, buy the best minced beef or steak or buy the meat and mince it yourself just before cooking. A true hamburger is simply meat plus a shake of pepper and salt. Many people feel that salt is a mistake for it draws out the meat juices but I like food well-seasoned during cooking.

Handle the meat mixture as lightly as possible and make the hamburgers in true American style – at least 1.5 cm/½ inch in thickness.

You can add many adornments in the form of salad, onion rings, pickles or chutney or tomato ketchup when the hamburger is served.

450 g/1 lb minced beef
salt and freshly ground black pepper

Blend the meat and seasonings. Form into 4 round cakes.
To fry: If there is a reasonable percentage of fat in the meat, you can cook the hamburgers without adding fat to the pan. Simply heat a heavy frying pan, put in the hamburgers and cook for 2 to 3 minutes on either side. If the meat is lean, grease the pan with a little butter, oil or fat to give a thin film. Heat, then add the hamburgers and cook for 2 to 3 minutes on either side. Serve in toasted sesame buns or soft rolls.
To grill: Preheat the grill, place a piece of foil on the grill pan and cook the hamburgers for 2 to 3 minutes on each side. Serve as above.

To make a change
Hamburgers in a Collar: Shape the meat into 4 round cakes. Derind 4 rashers of streaky bacon and stretch the bacon with the back of a knife to make it pliable. Wrap the bacon around the sides of the hamburgers and secure with wooden cocktail sticks or toothpicks. Place into a greased dish and cook in a preheated oven, set to 220°C/425°F, Gas Mark 7, for 5 to 6 minutes, or until the bacon is crisp and the meat is cooked. Remove the sticks or toothpicks and serve the hamburgers in toasted buns or rolls or with a mixture of vegetables or a mixed salad.
Hamburgers au Gratin: Top the cooked hamburgers with a thick layer of grated cheese. Place under a preheated grill until the cheese melts and turns golden.

Carpet Bag Steak

This Australian speciality is deliciously simple. Australians tend to cook one large steak as a joint, *see* **To make a change** below. I prefer to buy individual steaks, so each person can enjoy the meat cooked as they like it. Buy thick steaks, so you can cut pockets in the meat. You could use mussels or scallops instead of oysters.

> **4 rump or fillet steaks**
> *For the stuffing:*
> **100 g/4 oz button mushrooms**
> **8 oysters (12 if small)** *see* **method***
> **50 g/2 oz butter**
> **75 g/3 oz soft white breadcrumbs**
> **1 tablespoon chopped parsley**
> **salt and freshly ground black pepper**
> **1 teaspoon finely grated lemon zest**
> **1 tablespoon lemon juice**
> **1 egg**

Wipe and slice the mushrooms. *Slice the oysters (or leave them whole if small and allow 3 rather than 2 per person). Heat the butter and cook the mushrooms for several minutes, then blend with the rest of the stuffing ingredients. Make deep cuts in the sides of the steaks. Press the stuffing into these pockets and secure with toothpicks. Brush the meat with melted butter and grill or heat a little butter in a frying pan and cook the steaks. A rare steak needs about 2 to 3 minutes on each side, a medium-cooked steak 3 to 4 minutes on each side and a well-cooked steak 4 to 5 minutes on each side. Serve with a salad or mixed vegetables.

To make a change
Whole Carpet Bag Steak: Buy one large rump steak; allow 175 to 225 g/6 to 8 oz per person. Make cuts in the steak – one for each person. Put in the stuffing made as above. Place in a buttered dish, spread butter over the meat. Cook in a preheated oven set to 220°C/425°F, Gas Mark 7. Allow 20 minutes at this temperature, then lower the heat to 190°C/375°F, Gas Mark 5, and allow an extra 5 to 8 minutes per 450 g/1 lb, depending upon how well done you like the meat to be. Cut the steak so each person has a helping of the stuffing.

Meatballs

Many countries use minced meat to make meatballs and each country adds its own special flavourings. Fricadelles is the classic name for meatballs but in many countries they are called Fricadeller.

The following are delicious as cocktail savouries; they are based on a technique I learned in Holland. The addition of gelatine lets you mould the mixture when it is cold and subsequently melts when the balls are heated to give a lovely, moist, succulent texture.

> 1 medium onion
> 25 g/1 oz butter
> 1 teaspoon gelatine
> 2 tablespoons beef stock
> 450 g/1 lb minced beef
> 50 g/2 oz soft breadcrumbs
> pinch allspice
> 1 tablespoon chopped parsley
> salt and freshly ground black pepper
> 1 egg
> *For coating:*
> 25 g/1 oz flour
> *For frying:*
> oil or fat

Peel and chop or grate the onion. Heat the butter and fry the onion until soft. Sprinkle the gelatine on to the cold beef stock. Stand for 2 to 3 minutes then dissolve in the microwave or over a pan of very hot water. Mix the onion, gelatine and beef with the rest of the ingredients. Chill the mixture well then roll into tiny balls, about the size of an olive. Coat the balls with the flour and fry for a few minutes in very hot oil or fat. Drain on kitchen paper and put on to cocktail sticks. Serve at once.

To make a change
Fricadeller: Scandinavian countries make a lot of meat balls. Use the recipe above, but omit the gelatine. Make balls about the size of walnuts; coat with flour and poach gently in seasoned stock for 15 minutes. Thicken the stock with a little flour then add a knob of butter and a little cream to enrich it. Serve as a sauce.

Surprise Toad-in-the-Hole

Toad-in-the-Hole is considered homely fare but once it was a very much more lordly dish, containing lamb cutlets, lambs' kidneys and bacon as well as the familiar sausages. My mother used to add whatever oddments of meat she had available, which is why our Toad was always a surprise!

The golden rule for a really good Toad-in-the-Hole, whatever the filling, is that the sausages, or other fillings, must be well heated first and the oven temperature must be very high for the first few minutes of cooking time once the batter has been added.

For the batter:
110 g/4 oz plain flour
pinch salt
2 eggs
275 ml/9 fl oz milk or milk and water
For the filling:
25 g/1 oz fat
450 g/1 lb sausages or a mixture of diced
  skinned kidneys, sausages, diced bacon, etc.

Blend the ingredients together for the batter. Place the fat in the dish or tin and heat for a few minutes in the preheated oven, set to 200°C/400°F, Gas Mark 6. Add the sausages, or other fillings, turn in the fat and heat thoroughly for 5 to 8 minutes. Raise the oven setting to 230°C/450°F, Gas Mark 8. Whisk the batter and pour over the hot foods. Cook for 10 minutes, or until the batter has risen, then return the heat to 200°C/400°F, Gas Mark 6, and continue cooking for a further 20 minutes. Serve as soon as the food is cooked with mixed vegetables.

To make a change
Vegetarian Toad-in-the-Hole: Use cooked beans of various kinds, together with sliced courgettes and aubergines. Add 50 g/2 oz nuts or grated cheese to the batter. Heat the beans and other foods in vegetarian fat, exactly as above, add the batter and continue cooking as the recipe. Serve with well seasoned, home-made tomato purée.
Popovers: Make the batter with 175 ml/6 fl oz liquid only. Grease muffin tins and heat as above. Spoon in the batter and cook at the setting given for 15 minutes. Fill with cooked meats or vegetables.

Bobotie

This is a traditional South African dish and a splendid way to use minced lamb or beef. I have demonstrated this to audiences and enjoy the look of amazement on their faces when I announce I shall be topping the savoury meat mixture with custard! It is, of course, a savoury topping.

1 slice of bread, about 50 g/2 oz in weight
300 ml/½ pint milk
2 medium onions
50 g/2 oz butter or margarine
1 tablespoon mild curry powder, or to taste
550 g/1¼ lb good quality minced lamb or beef
1 to 2 tablespoons lemon juice
2 teaspoons brown sugar
salt and freshly ground black pepper
25 to 50 g/1 to 2 oz blanched almonds
2 eggs
2 fresh or 1 dried bay leaf

Put the bread into a bowl, add the cold milk and leave for 10 minutes, then strain the milk and put on one side. Peel and finely chop the onions. Heat the butter or margarine and cook the onions until soft. Stir in the curry powder towards the end of the cooking time and blend with the onions. Add the meat to the pan, and stir over a low heat for about 10 minutes, or until the meat changes colour.

Mix the softened bread with the onion and meat mixture. Add lemon juice, sugar and seasoning to taste. Spread into a 1.2 litre/2 pint casserole or ovenproof dish. Arrange the almonds on top. Whisk the eggs with the milk left from soaking the bread. Strain over the top of the meat. Add the bay leaves or leaf. Bake for 40 minutes in a preheated oven, set to 160°C/325°F, Gas Mark 3. Cover the top of the dish after 25 minutes, if the custard mixture is over-browning. Remove the bay leaves or leaf. Serve with mixed vegetables or rice and a salad.

To make a change
Add 50 g/2 oz chopped tenderized or cooked dried apricots to the meat mixture as well as the almonds. If you prefer a deeper custard layer, use 450 ml/¾ pint milk.

Liver Dumplings

This recipe dates back to the war years when a slice of liver was a treat. The amount obtainable was very small so ways of making it go further were very popular. The original recipe was given to the home economists at the Ministry of Food by helpful Czech cooks. Needless to say in those days the dumplings were cooked in water, not stock.

> 225 g/8 oz lambs' liver
> 175 g/6 oz self-raising flour
> salt and freshly ground black pepper
> pinch dry mustard powder
> 50 g/2 oz butter or margarine
> water to bind
> *To cook the dumplings:*
> 1 litre/1¾ pints lamb or beef stock or water

Mince or chop the liver very finely. Sift the flour and seasonings into a bowl, rub in the butter or margarine, add the liver and blend well. Gradually add enough water to make a soft, rolling consistency. Divide the slightly sticky mixture into 12 portions. Roll into balls with floured fingers.

Bring the stock or water to boiling point. Drop in the dumplings and cook fairly rapidly for about 15 minutes or until well-risen. Lift from the liquid with a perforated spoon and serve. Some of the stock can be thickened, flavoured with port wine, and made into a sauce to serve with the dumplings, or top them with melted butter and chopped parsley. The dumpling mixture can be flavoured with chopped parsley too.

To make a change
Liver Soufflé: Mince 175 g/6 oz lambs' or calves' liver. Heat 25 g/1 oz butter or margarine in a saucepan, stir in 25 g/1 oz flour, then gradually add 150 ml/¼ pint and stir as the sauce comes to the boil and makes a thick consistency – known as a *panada*. Add the liver with a little salt, freshly ground black pepper and 1 teaspoon French mustard. If you like a soft-textured soufflé stir in 2 tablespoons double cream. Separate 3 eggs and beat the yolks into the liver mixture. Whisk the whites until they stand in *soft* peaks. Fold into the other ingredients. Bake for 30 minutes, or until well-risen and firm, in a preheated oven set to 190°C/375°F, Gas Mark 5. Serve at once.

Goulasch

These days when quickly prepared dishes are the order of the day, it's easy to forget just how delicious a good stew can be. A genuine Goulasch or *Gulyas*, with its mixture of meats and paprika flavouring, is surely one of the best stews. It can be cooked one day, allowed to cool, then reheated thoroughly the next day, when it tastes even better. If you are reheating the mixture, you will need to add just a little more liquid.

Be careful when using paprika. It is a spice that deteriorates quickly in storage and tastes musty when stale.

> 675 g/1½ lb meat, preferably 225 g/8 oz
> stewing beef, 225 g/8 oz stewing veal and
> 225 g/8 oz lean pork
> 450 g/1 lb onions
> 50 g/2 oz butter or margarine or other fat
> 675 g/1½ lb plum tomatoes or use canned
> tomatoes
> 1 to 2 tablespoons paprika, according to taste
> salt and freshly ground black pepper
> veal or beef stock, if required, *see* method
> 450 g/1 lb potatoes, weight when peeled
> *To garnish:*
> yoghurt
> chopped parsley

Cut the meat into neat pieces. Peel and thinly slice the onions. Heat the butter, margarine or fat and gently cook the onions for 2 to 3 minutes. Meanwhile liquidize the tomatoes to make a purée.

Add the meats to the onions in the pan and continue cooking until pale golden. Blend in the paprika with the salt and pepper and stir gently over the heat for a few minutes – paprika burns easily.

Pour in the tomato purée. Cover the pan and simmer gently for 1 hour. Check during this time that you have sufficient liquid in the pan. If not add more tomato purée or a little stock. This should be a thick stew but there must be sufficient liquid before adding the potatoes.

Thickly slice the potatoes, add to the pan and continue cooking for a further 45 minutes, or until the meat is tender. Serve topped with yoghurt and plenty of chopped parsley. **Serves 4 to 6**

Bredie

This is a traditional South African stew made of mutton or lamb. In one version I tasted, the dish was flavoured with special flowers called *waterblommetjie*. As these are unobtainable elsewhere, I use rosemary. Mutton is difficult to obtain these days, so I use breast of lamb. As this cut is fatty, you may prefer to use lean loin chops instead. If using breast meat I suggest you cook the Bredie one day, allow it to cool, then refrigerate it. Next day remove the fat from the top of the stew before reheating.

> **2 breasts of lamb, weighing about 1.3 kg/3 lb or**
>   **8 lamb chops**
> **pinch ground ginger, optional**
> **salt and freshly ground black pepper**
> **1 to 2 teaspoons brown sugar, *see* method***
> **25 g/1 oz flour**
> **2 medium onions**
> **1 medium cooking apple**
> **450 g/1 lb tomatoes**
> **1 to 2 tablespoons oil, *see* method****
> **300 ml/½ pint lamb stock**
> **1 to 2 teaspoon chopped rosemary or**
> **½ teaspoon dried rosemary**

Cut the breast of lamb into small pieces, or ask the butcher to do this for you. Blend the ginger, if used, with the seasoning, sugar and flour.

*It is a good idea to use the larger amount of sugar with the fatter breast of lamb. Coat the meat in this mixture.

Peel and thinly slice the onions and apple; skin and chop the tomatoes. Heat the oil in a large pan. **Use the smaller amount with breast of lamb, or if there is a fair amount of fat on the lamb chops. Fry the meat in the hot oil until golden on both sides, then remove from the pan on to a plate. Add the onions and apple and turn in any oil remaining in the pan until these are slightly golden in colour.

Return the meat to the pan with tomatoes, stock and rosemary, stir well, then put the lid on the saucepan. If this is a poor fit place a piece of foil underneath, as it's important that the small amount of liquid does not boil away. Simmer for 2 hours for breast of lamb, or 1¼ hours for lamb chops. Serve with seasonal vegetables.

Crown Roast of Lamb

My reason for including this dish, is that I find it one of the simplest ways of turning meat into an impressive main dish. Best end of neck of lamb (rack) is surely one of the most succulent of joints.

The stuffing, which is cooked with the meat, adds flavour and helps to keep the meat moist during the cooking process. One rather unusual stuffing is suggested below, but most flavourings blend well with lamb. If you are not fond of stuffings, you can fill the centre of the crown with beautifully cooked vegetables just before serving.

Take care to protect the ends of the bones and the top of the stuffing during cooking, so they do not burn.

2 racks of lamb, each with at least 6 chops
For the pepper and citrus stuffing:
1 green pepper
1 red pepper
2 large oranges
1 lime or small lemon
2 tablespoons finely chopped chives
**75 g/3 oz soft white breadcrumbs or cooked
  rice**
50 g/2 oz butter or margarine
50 g/2 oz raisins
salt and freshly ground black pepper
pinch paprika
50 g/2 oz pine nuts
To garnish:
mint or watercress sprigs

A butcher will prepare the crown for you, given reasonable notice. If you have to do this yourself ask for the joints to be chined (cut between the chops) so the meat may be made into a round. Trim the fat away from the ends of the bones. Sew the sides of the joints together to make the round, using fine string. Place on a piece of foil; this makes it easy to weigh when stuffed and if any stuffing falls out during cooking it is easy to spoon on to the dish from the foil.

Deseed and dice the peppers. Grate a little zest from the oranges and lime or lemon, discard the rest of the peel and pith and chop the segments of fruit. Mix the peppers, fruit zest and chopped segments with the stuffing ingredients. Put into the centre of the joint. Weigh the joint, then cover the top of the stuffing and bone ends with foil. Nowadays most people like lamb fairly pink, so allow barely 20 minutes per 450 g/1 lb and about 15 minutes over, in a preheated oven set to 200°C/400°F, Gas Mark 6. For well-cooked lamb allow the full 20 minutes per 450 g/1 lb and 20 minutes over. Remove the foil from the top of the stuffing for the last 15 minutes cooking time. Garnish the bone ends with cutlet frills; add the sprigs of mint or watercress to the dish.

To carve the meat: discard the string, cut down between the bones and allow at least 2 cutlets per person, with a portion of stuffing.

The meat and fat removed from the ends of the bones can be simmered in water to make good stock for the gravy. This is more interesting if flavoured with a good squeeze of lime or lemon juice, orange juice and a little sweet sherry.

Escalopes

Fillets of veal are the most usual source of escalopes but they can also be made from lean fillet slices of pork and lamb. The breast meat from turkey or chicken is excellent for this purpose. Like veal, poultry escalopes are very lean, so be reasonably generous with the amount of fat used and take care that the meat is not overcooked.

If the slices of meat or poultry are too thick for your taste, make them thinner by beating them gently with a rolling pin or a meat hammer. Protect the meat by putting it between greaseproof or waxed paper. In this way the fibres are not broken.

Fried Escalopes: Coat the meat in seasoned flour, beaten egg and fine breadcrumbs. Crisp breadcrumbs can be used since the cooking time is short. For 4 escalopes you need at least 75 g/3 oz butter plus a tablespoon of sunflower oil (this helps to prevent the butter from burning). Fry quickly on each side until golden, reduce the heat and cook more slowly until the meat is cooked. Drain and garnish with lemon slices and chopped parsley or chopped hard-boiled egg and parsley. Anchovy fillets make another classic garnish.

Cooked escalopes can be topped with fried eggs and garnished with capers and small pickled gherkins or they can be topped with slices of lean ham and Gruyère cheese and browned under a preheated grill.

Tajine Tfaia

Tajine recipes vary in the choice of vegetables used with the lamb. Mutton, chicken joints, or tender beef, can be used instead of lamb. The meat is partially cooked in a saucepan, then transferred, with extra flavourings, to the pot or casserole. Cooking is completed in the oven.

> 450 to 550 g/1 to 1¼ lb lamb, cut from the leg
>   or shoulder
> pinch ground cumin
> pinch powdered saffron or a few saffron
>   strands
> pinch ground ginger
> pinch ground coriander
> 2 teaspoons finely grated lemon zest
> salt and freshly ground black pepper
> 2 medium onions
> 2 garlic cloves
> a little water
> 50 g/2 oz butter or 2 tablespoons olive oil
> 100 g/4 oz blanched almonds

Cut the meat into 3.5 cm/1½ inch pieces. Blend the spices with the lemon zest and seasoning and coat the meat. Peel and finely chop the onions and garlic. Put the meat with half the onions and garlic into a saucepan. Add the water, cover the pan and simmer for 40 minutes or until the meat is half cooked. Meanwhile heat the butter or oil and cook the almonds until golden brown. Remove from the pan, add the remaining onion and garlic and cook for 5 minutes. Transfer the meat and liquid to a casserole and add the onions, garlic and almonds. Use only enough liquid to moisten the meat and onions. Cover tightly and continue cooking for 40 minutes in the preheated oven set to 190°C/375°F, Gas Mark 5. Serve with rice or couscous, see page 125.

To make a change
Tajine Qamama: Blend 1 tablespoon of honey with the liquid. Other recipes add tomato purée, or cooked beans, or cooked spinach, or hard-boiled eggs or grated cheese plus a few breadcrumbs to the meat when placed into the casserole to complete the cooking process.

Couscous

In Arab countries there are special utensils for cooking couscous; but I find muslin placed on the base and sides of a steamer a good substitute. Make sure the steamer fits tightly on the saucepan.

> **675 g/1½ lb lamb or chicken, weight when**
>   **boned**
> *For the vegetable mixture:*
> **350 g/12 oz carrots; 225 g/8 oz turnips**
> **225 g/8 oz courgettes; 100 g/4 oz green beans**
> **2 large tomatoes; 3 medium onions**
> **2 tablespoons olive oil**
> **water,** *see* **method**
> **pinch powdered saffron or several saffron**
>   **strands**
> **pinch Ras el Hanout,** *see* **page 133**
> **2 tablespoons chopped parsley**
> **salt and freshly ground black pepper**
> **300 g/10 oz couscous (coarse semolina)**
> **100 g/4 oz seedless raisins or other dried fruit**
> **50 g/2 oz butter**

Dice the lamb or chicken and prepared vegetables. Heat the oil, add the meat or chicken and the onions. Cook for a few minutes. Add water to cover plus a quarter of the vegetables, the saffron, spice, parsley and seasoning. Cover the pan and cook for 20 minutes. Meanwhile soak the couscous in cold water with a pinch of salt for 15 minutes then strain. Spoon half over the muslin. Place the steamer on the saucepan, cover and cook for 4 minutes or until the couscous is moistened with the steam. Add the rest of the couscous. Cover again and cook for 20 minutes. Put the remaining vegetables into the saucepan with the dried fruit and extra seasoning. Cook for 30 minutes. Continue cooking the couscous.

Tip the couscous into a hot bowl, turn with two spoons, to separate the grains; blend in the butter. Arrange in a ring on a hot dish; spoon the meat or chicken, the vegetables and dried fruit into the centre.

Hot sauce: Blend 2 crushed garlic cloves, 1 teaspoon of chilli powder, 3 tablespoons of chopped red pepper into 300 ml/½ pint of the stock. Serve with the couscous. *Serves 6*

Navarin of Lamb

The interesting caramel flavour characterizes this stew, but it must not be so strong that it disguises the taste of the meat. It is therefore important to check the browning of the meat and the vegetables carefully, and to use a saucepan with a thick base, so that the food does not burn. This dish is delicious when young, early summer vegetables are in season.

> 450 to 550 g/1 to 1¼ lb lamb, cut from the leg
>   or shoulder
> salt and freshly ground black pepper
> 8 shallots or very small onions
> 8 to 12 small carrots or 4 to 6 larger ones
> 2 small turnips or 1 larger one
> 450 g/1 lb potatoes, preferably small and new
> 50 g/2 oz butter
> 1 tablespoon caster sugar
> 1 tablespoon flour
> 450 ml/¾ pint lamb stock
> bouquet garni (sprig of parsley, chives,
>   rosemary and mint, tied in cotton)

Cut the meat into 3.5 cm/1½ inch pieces and season lightly. Peel the shallots or onions, carrots, turnip(s) and scrape, or peel, the potatoes (keep these in cold water until ready to cook). If using larger carrots and turnip cut these into neat pieces. Large old potatoes should be cut into 2 cm/¾ inch slices.

Heat the butter in a large saucepan. Add the seasoned meat together with half the sugar. Turn in the butter until the meat becomes a golden brown and there is a faint smell of caramel. Remove from the pan. Add the shallots or onions, carrots and turnips, together with the rest of the sugar and heat gently, stirring all the time until golden in colour and lightly caramelized. Remove from the pan. Stir in the flour and cook gently, stirring all the time, until brown in colour.

Add the stock, herbs, meat and vegetables, with the exception of the potatoes. Cover the pan and cook steadily for 40 minutes. Put in the potatoes and blend with the rest of the ingredients. Continue cooking gently for 30 to 40 minutes, until the potatoes are soft, but unbroken. Remove the herbs and serve the Navarin with a green vegetable.

Pork with Satay Sauce

Satay sauces, based on nuts with the addition of spices and peanut butter, are a delicious accompaniment to meat.

> **550 g/1¼ lb lean pork**
> *For the marinade and sauce*:
> **2 small onions**
> **2 garlic cloves**
> **2 teaspoons grated lemon zest or chopped**
>   **lemon grass**
> **1 tablespoon sunflower oil**
> **2 tablespoons soy sauce**
> **½ teaspoon ground coriander**
> **pinch chilli powder**
> **3 tablespoons peanut butter**
> **175 g/6 oz roasted peanuts**
> **150 m/¼ pint coconut milk, see page 129**
> **1 tablespoon lemon juice**
> **1 tablespoon brown sugar**
> **salt and freshly ground black pepper**

Cut the pork into small dice and put into a dish. Peel and chop the onions and garlic and add to the pork with the lemon zest or grass, the oil, 1 tablespoon of the soy sauce together with the coriander and chilli powder. Turn the pork in this mixture and leave for 1 hour so that the meat absorbs the flavours. Turn over once or twice during this time.

Lift the meat from this mixture and thread on to bamboo skewers then cook over a very hot barbecue or under a preheated grill until tender.

While the meat is marinating prepare the sauce. Put the peanut butter, peanuts and coconut milk into a food processor or liquidizer and add the lemon juice, sugar and a little seasoning together with the remaining soy sauce. Liquidize until a smooth thick, mixture. Dilute with a little more coconut milk or boiling water if a thinner mixture is required. Heat the sauce and serve with the meat and cooked rice.

To make a change
Diced chicken or beef are equally good in this recipe; marinate with the same flavourings.

Sweet and Sour Pork with Water Chestnuts

This recipe produces a pleasant blend of sweet and sour flavours and a sauce which is not too thick. The canned water chestnuts should be well-drained and added at the last minute so they retain their firm texture.

550 g/1¼ lb lean pork
3 teaspoons cornflour
salt and freshly ground black pepper
1 red pepper
1 small can pineapple rings in syrup
1 small can water chestnuts
2 tablespoons sunflower oil
6 tablespoons chopped spring onions
2 tablespoons white wine vinegar
1 tablespoon rice wine or dry sherry
1 tablespoon brown sugar
1 tablespoon soy sauce

Cut the pork into 2 cm/¾ inch dice. Put into a bowl and sprinkle with 2 teaspoons of the cornflour and a little salt and pepper. Stir well, so that the meat absorbs the cornflour and seasoning.

Deseed and dice the pepper. Drain the pineapple. Put 150 ml/¼ pint of the syrup on one side. Cut the pineapple rings into small pieces. Drain and dice the water chestnuts.

Heat the oil in a wok or frying pan and stir-fry the pork steadily for 10 minutes. Add the red pepper and spring onions. Stir-fry for 2 minutes then pour in the vinegar, wine or sherry and continue stirring over the heat for 2 minutes.

Blend the remaining teaspoon of cornflour with the pineapple syrup and add to the wok or frying pan with the sugar and soy sauce. Stir as the mixture thickens slightly and continue cooking for 5 minutes.

Add the water chestnuts, heat well and serve with cooked rice.

To make a change
Sweet and Sour Chicken: Use diced chicken instead of pork. Omit the water chestnuts, otherwise follow the recipe above. Add 2 teaspoons of finely diced fresh ginger to the sauce. Stir 100 g/4 oz of peeled prawns into the sauce towards the end of the cooking period.

Chicken Chop (Curry)

This is the strange name given to a chicken curry served in West Africa. My husband discovered it when he was out there with the RAF. I can't guarantee that these were the exact ingredients used at the time. Be warned, it's hot! Cut down on the chilli and ginger if you prefer a milder taste.

> 1 chicken, weighing 1.8 kg/4 lb
> 2 onions
> 1 small lemon
> 2 tablespoons groundnut or sunflower oil
> *To flavour the curry:*
> 1 large red chilli pepper or ½ teaspoon chilli
>   powder
> ¼ teaspoon cayenne pepper
> ½ teaspoon turmeric
> 2 tablespoons grated fresh ginger
> 300 ml/½ pint chicken stock
> 300 ml/½ pint fresh coconut milk, or *see*
>   method using creamed coconut
> 5 cm/2 inch piece of cinnamon stick
> salt and freshly ground black pepper
> 100 g/4 oz fresh dates (weight when stoned)

Cut the chicken into small joints. Peel and chop the onions, grate the lemon zest and squeeze out the juice. Heat the oil and fry the chicken with the onions until pale golden. Remove from the pan. Chop the red chilli pepper and mix with the cayenne, turmeric and ginger. Add to the pan, then blend in the chicken stock. Return the chicken and onions to the pan with the lemon rind and half the lemon juice.

To make the coconut milk: Halve a fresh coconut, cut out the white flesh and grate it. Pour 300 ml/½ pint boiling water over this, leave until cold; put into muslin. Squeeze hard to extract as much flavour as possible. If using creamed coconut, add 75 g/3 oz to the boiling water and stir until dissolved. Put the coconut milk, cinnamon stick, seasoning and dates into the pan. Stir well to blend. Cover the pan tightly, lower the heat and simmer for 2 hours. Remove the cinnamon and add more lemon juice if required. Serve with cooked rice, a sweet chutney and a few extra dates.

Chicken Pie

Under the unusual herb-flavoured pastry of this pie the chicken and other ingredients nestle in a delicately spiced creamy sauce.

For the pastry:
225 g/8 oz plain flour
pinch salt
110 g/4 oz butter or other fat(s)
1 tablespoon very finely chopped parsley
½ teaspoon very finely chopped thyme
1 teaspoon very finely chopped lemon zest
water to bind
For the filling:
1 chicken, weighing 1.8 kg/4 lb, or 4 large
  chicken breast portions
150 ml/¼ pint chicken stock, *see* method
50 g/2 oz chicken fat or butter, *see* method
2 medium onions
175 g/6 oz small button mushrooms
25 g/1 oz flour
pinch powdered saffron or several saffron
  strands
pinch mixed spice
salt and freshly ground black pepper
300 ml/½ pint double or whipping cream
To glaze:
1 egg

Sift the flour and salt. Rub in the fat, add the herbs, lemon zest and water to bind. Wrap the pastry and chill while preparing the filling.

Bone and skin the chicken. Cover the bones and skin with water. Simmer for 1 hour to make a really concentrated stock, measure out 150 ml/¼ pint. If made ahead and chilled, you will have fat on top to use in the sauce, so giving a more pronounced taste. Peel and chop the onions, wipe the mushrooms, cut the chicken into neat portions. Heat the butter or fat, gently fry the chicken with the onions until golden. Put into a 1.8 litre/3 pint pie dish with the mushrooms. Mix the flour, spices and seasoning, add to the fat remaining in the pan, then blend in the stock and just over half the cream. Stir as the sauce comes to the boil and thickens. Spoon over the chicken, allow to cool.

Roll out the pastry. Cover the filling and decorate with leaves of pastry. Make a good-sized hole in the centre of the pastry; place a piece of firm card or foil in this, so it will not close in cooking.

Beat the egg and brush over the pastry. Bake for 20 minutes in a preheated oven set to 200°C/400°F, Gas Mark 6. Lower the heat to 160°C/325°F, Gas Mark 3, and continue cooking for a further 1 hour. If the pastry is browning too fast, cover with greaseproof paper or foil.

When the pie is cooked remove the card or foil from the slit in the pastry; insert a small funnel into this and pour in the rest of the cream; this could be warmed before adding. The pie is equally good hot or cold.

Serves 6

Chicken with Olives and Lemon

This is an excellent way of giving flavour to chicken portions.

> **1 lemon**
> **75 g/3 oz butter**
> **salt and freshly ground black pepper**
> **4 chicken portions**
> **3 tablespoons black or green olives**

Grate the zest from the lemon, blend with the butter and heat in a large frying pan. Season the chicken and cook steadily in the butter until tender, add lemon juice to taste and the olives, heat for a few minutes then serve.

To make a change
Chicken in white wine: The sauce is thickened with plain chocolate, which gives a rich colour and flavour, without being too sweet.

Heat 25 g/1 oz of butter, add 1 finely chopped medium sized onion, cook for 5 minutes then remove from the pan. Add a further 50 g/2 oz of butter and cook 4 chicken breast portions until nearly tender. Return the onion to the pan with 300 ml/½ pint dry white wine, 1 tablespoon tomato purée (paste), 50 g/2 oz plain chocolate, a little seasoning and ½ teaspoon chopped thyme. Stir until the chocolate has melted, cover the pan and simmer gently for 10 minutes.

Djaja Mammra

This recipe uses an interesting Arab stuffing with chicken. The bird can be simmered in liquid in a saucepan or roasted in the oven. Both methods of cooking are explained here. The stuffing is excellent for a turkey or even small birds, like quail, *see* page 133.

If using frozen poultry or game, make quite sure that the birds are completely defrosted before cooking. Place the stuffing in the neck end only of the bird, rather than the body cavity, because the moist stuffing can prevent the bird cooking properly. In the case of quail you will have to put the stuffing into the body, as the neck end is too small.

For the stuffing:
75 g/3 oz cooked couscous, *see* page 125, or
  cooked rice
25 g/1 oz butter
50 g/2 oz blanched almonds
100 g/4 oz seedless raisins
pinch Ras el Hanout*
salt and freshly ground black pepper

25 to 50 g/1 to 2 oz butter to coat the chicken
1 roasting chicken, about 2.25 kg/5 lb in weight
ingredients for cooking in water, *see* method

Put the couscous or rice into a bowl. Melt the butter. Blend with the couscous or rice and the other ingredients for the stuffing. Put into the neck end of the bird. Pull the skin over the stuffing and secure with wooden cocktail sticks or toothpicks. Soften the butter for coating the bird.

To cook in liquid: Peel and slice 2 onions. Put into a large saucepan. Spread 25 g/1 oz butter over the chicken breast. Add water to half-cover the coated bird together with a sprig of thyme, a sprig of parsley, a pinch of powdered saffron or several saffron strands. Cover the pan and simmer for 1¼ hours or until the chicken is cooked. Remove the bird and place on to a heated dish. Strain 450 ml/¾ pint of the stock.

Blend 150 ml/¼ pint milk with 25 g/1 oz cornflour. Put into a saucepan with the stock, stir as the mixture comes to the boil and thickens, then add 150 ml/¼ pint single cream and any seasoning required. Carve the chicken, serve with the sauce and mixed vegetables.

To roast: Put the stuffing into the neck end of the bird and secure as described above. Spread 50 g/2 oz softened butter over the bird and weigh this after adding the stuffing. Place into a roasting tin.

If cooking a fresh bird, preheat the oven to 200°C/400°F, Gas Mark 6, and allow 15 minutes per 450 g/1 lb and 15 minutes over. If cooking a defrosted frozen bird preheat the oven to 180°C/350°F, Gas Mark 4, and allow 22 minutes per 450 g/1 lb and 22 minutes over. The quality of birds varies, so always test just before the end of the cooking time by inserting the tip of a knife where the leg joins the body. If the juices that run out are pink the bird needs a little more cooking.

To roast turkey: Timings as above. Put the bird with the breast side downwards for the first half of the cooking time. For any weight over 5.4 kg/12 lb allow an extra 12 minutes per 450 g/1 lb at the higher setting or 18 to 20 minutes per 450 g/1 lb at the lower setting.

To roast game birds: Allow the same cooking time as for chicken. Quail needs 25 to 30 minutes at the higher temperature above.   **Serves 4 to 6**

* Ras el Hanout is a mixture of spices used in Moroccan cooking. If unavailable, blend equal amounts of curry powder, ground ginger, ground cinnamon and mixed spice plus a little cayenne pepper.

Lemon Chicken

If you want to give chicken a delicate but unusual flavour use 1 or 2 lemons.

1 roasting chicken, about 2.5 kg/5 lb in weight
1 large or 2 small lemons
25 to 50 g/1 to 2 oz butter, see method

The chicken can be cooked in liquid or roasted as described for Djaja Mammra above Cut the lemon or lemons in half and remove all the pips. Rub the cut surfaces over the whole of the chicken, then spread the breast with butter. Put the lemon(s) inside the bird. For a milder flavour remove most of the peel and white pith and simply add the centre of the fruit. If cooking in liquid, serve with the sauce given on p.132. As there is a good proportion of lemon juice in the stock, *do not* allow the mixture to boil when the milk and cream are added. An alternative method of making sauce is given on page 141.

Chicken Maryland

The combination of chicken, sweetcorn and bananas is very pleasant. The chicken can be coated with seasoned flour only; but it has a better appearance if flour, beaten egg and breadcrumbs are used.

4 chicken joints, either all breasts or all legs
salt and freshly ground black pepper
25 g/1 oz flour
1 egg
approximately 50 g/2 oz fine crisp breadcrumbs
For the sweetcorn fritters:
50 g/2 oz self-raising flour
salt and cayenne pepper
1 egg plus a little milk*
175 g/6 oz cooked or canned sweetcorn

4 small bananas
For frying:
4 tablespoons sunflower oil

Skin the chicken joints; season the flour and use half to coat the chicken. Beat the egg and brush over the chicken joints then coat in the breadcrumbs. Mix the ingredients together for the fritters. The mixture should drop easily from the spoon. *If necessary add a small amount of milk. Peel the bananas and coat in the remaining flour.

Heat half the oil then fry the chicken quickly until golden brown on all sides. Lower the heat and continue cooking for 10 minutes, or until tender. Heat the remaining oil in a second frying pan. Drop 4 portions of the fritter mixture into the oil. Fry quickly until golden brown on both sides then lower the heat and cook for a few more minutes. Towards the end of this period add the bananas.

Drain the food on kitchen paper and arrange on to a heated dish. Serve with green salad and new or creamed potatoes.

Note: To avoid too much frying, coat the chicken as above. Heat, then grease, a metal baking tray and place the chicken on it. Top with a light sprinkling of oil. Bake for 25 to 30 minutes in a preheated oven, set to 200°C/400°F, Gas Mark 6. Serve with heated bananas and cooked sweetcorn.

Roast Duck with Prune and Apple Stuffing

Fear not – roast duck is not greasy if the skin is pricked lightly during cooking.

> **2 medium ducks with giblets**
> *For the stuffing:*
> **175 g/6 oz lightly cooked prunes (weight when stoned)**
> **1 large cooking apple**
> **25 g/1 oz butter or margarine**
> **50 g/2 oz wholemeal breadcrumbs**
> **2 teaspoons chopped fresh sage or 1 teaspoon dried sage**
> **1 egg**
> **salt and freshly ground black pepper**
> *To garnish:*
> **lightly cooked prunes**

Defrost frozen birds completely, and dry them. Simmer the giblets in water to cover to make stock for the gravy. Drain and chop the prunes. Peel, core, then finely chop the apple. Melt the butter or margarine and mix with the prunes, apple and the remainder of the stuffing ingredients. Put under the skin at the neck end of the ducks and secure with wooden cocktail sticks or toothpicks. Weigh the birds singly. If one bird is slightly larger than the other put it into the oven a few minutes earlier. Place the ducks on a rack in the roasting tin. (This is important as it allows surplus fat to drain down into the tin.)

Follow the timings and temperatures given on page 133 for roasting fresh or frozen poultry. On the lower setting you may need to raise the temperature towards the end of cooking to give a crisp, brown skin.

The secret of crisp skin, and no excess fat on ducks, is to *lightly* prick the skin after 30 minutes cooking time and again after 1 hour; or 40 minutes and 1 hour 10 minutes, if using the lower oven temperature. This allows the surplus fat to spurt out; *heavy* pricking means the fat runs into the flesh. Goose should be cooked and pricked as duck.

Garnish the cooked ducks with the prunes and cut into neat portions.

Serve with gravy, made as the sauce on page 141. Add the *beurre-manie* to the duck stock. Flavour with port wine if desired.   ***Serves 4 to 6***

Salmis of Grouse

'Salmis' means lightly roasted game or poultry, which is then reheated in a wine sauce. The word is believed to date from the 14th century. Follow this recipe for any game birds or poultry. Make quite sure the birds are *not* overcooked when roasting or reheating.

> **2 lightly roasted young grouse**
> **100 g/4 oz cooked ham, cut in one slice**
> **1 medium onion or 2 shallots**
> **3 medium carrots**
> **100 g/4 oz button mushrooms**
> **75 g/3 oz dripping from roasting the birds, or**
> **butter**
> **40 g/1½ oz flour**
> **600 ml/1 pint game stock, made by simmering**
> **giblets**
> **150 ml/¼ pint sweet sherry or a Madeira wine**
> **2 teaspoons chopped chervil or parsley**
> **1 bay leaf**
> **pinch ground mace**
> **salt and pepper**
> **2 tablespoons glacé* cherries**
> *To garnish:*
> **small fried croûtons of bread****
> **2 tablespoons glacé* cherries**

Skin and joint the grouse. Dice the ham. Peel and roughly chop the onion or shallots and the carrots. Wipe the mushrooms. Heat the dripping or butter in a saucepan. Fry the vegetables for 5 minutes. Stir in the flour and cook gently for 2 to 3 minutes. Gradually blend in the stock and sherry or Madeira; stir as the sauce comes to the boil and thickens. Add the herbs, mace and seasoning. Cover the pan and simmer for 10 minutes. Remove the bay leaf then sieve or liquidize the mixture. If it is too thick, add extra stock, then pour into a large saucepan.

Add the grouse, ham and cherries. Heat gently for 20 minutes. Garnish with the fried croûtons and cherries. *Serves 4 to 6*

* known as candied cherries in America.
** small shapes of bread, fried in fat or oil, then well drained.

Pigeon and Mushroom Ragoût

Pigeons have a very good flavour, especially when young and tender. At that stage they are known as *squabs*. Select birds in the usual way – the flesh should be plump and the legs pliable. Here are two quite different ways of cooking the birds. Other game birds could be used instead.

> **4 young pigeons (squabs)**
> **300 g/10 oz large button or wild mushrooms**
> **2 large tomatoes**
> **50 g/2 oz butter or margarine**
> **25 g/1 oz flour**
> **600 ml/1 pint game or beef stock**
> **salt and freshly ground black pepper**
> **2 tablespoons redcurrant jelly**
> **3 tablespoons red wine**
> *To garnish:*
> **fried croûtons of bread,** *see* **page 136**
> **few glacé cherries and watercress**

Halve the pigeons. Wipe the mushrooms. Skin, deseed and chop the tomatoes. Heat the butter or margarine in a large saucepan and fry the pigeons for a few minutes. Remove these from the pan. Stir in the flour and cook gently until this turns golden brown, then blend in the stock. Bring to the boil, and allow the liquid to thicken slightly, then add the pigeons, mushrooms, tomatoes and a little seasoning. Cover the saucepan and simmer gently for 1 hour, or until the birds are tender. Remove these and the mushrooms from the liquid with a perforated spoon and place on a heated dish. Sieve or liquidize the liquid, then return to the saucepan with the jelly and wine and heat. Serve with the pigeons. Garnish the birds with the croûtons, cherries and watercress.

To make a change
Pigeon Cutlets: Halve 4 small pigeons and remove as many bones as possible. Blend a little chopped bacon with 225 g/8 oz pork sausage meat. Press against the cut sides of the pigeons. Coat in seasoned flour, then beaten egg and fine breadcrumbs. Fry quickly in hot oil or fat, until golden, then lower the heat and continue cooking for a further 10 minutes. Drain and serve with a crisp salad.

137

SAVOURIES & SALADS

According to my family, I am a vegetable addict, and it's true that I enjoy cooking and eating vegetables very much. Nowadays, it's relatively easy to obtain a wide range of vegetables that can be cooked in all kinds of different ways to serve with meat or fish, or as a dish in their own right. Choose vegetables with a critical eye: check they really are fresh and cook them with loving care, so that they retain their texture as well as their flavour.

Cheesey Potatoes

Served with an interesting salad, this is excellent as a light lunch or supper dish. The potatoes need to be creamed carefully, so they are really light and smooth. There is a saying, 'A potato boiled, is a potato spoiled'. Too speedy cooking breaks the outside of the potatoes before they are cooked in the centre.

    The following recipe is equally good with mashed carrots, cauliflower or celeriac.

> 450 g/1 lb old potatoes (weight when peeled)
> salt and freshly ground black pepper
> 25 g/1 oz butter or margarine
> 3 tablespoons milk
> 150 g/5 oz Cheddar cheese
> 3 eggs
> 1 tablespoon finely chopped parsley
> 1 tablespoon finely chopped chives

Peel the potatoes and place into boiling salted water. Cover the pan and cook steadily until just soft, then strain and mash. Heat the butter or margarine with the milk; add to the potatoes and beat vigorously. Grate the cheese and separate the eggs. Beat most of the cheese, the egg yolks and herbs into the potatoes with any extra seasoning required. Whisk the egg whites until just stiff; fold into the potato mixture. Spoon into a greased 20 cm/8 inch soufflé dish. Top with the last of the cheese and bake for 30 minutes in a preheated oven, set to 190°C/375°F, Gas Mark 5. Serve at once.

Macaroni Soufflé

Until the sixties, macaroni cheese was one of the very few pasta dishes cooked in Britain. The first recipe on this page was created to make this classic dish more interesting. Today, various kinds of pasta – dried, fresh and home-made – are enjoyed by a great many people. Pasta is very nutritious and blends with an unlimited range of other ingredients.

> 75 g/3 oz short length macaroni
> salt and freshly ground black pepper
> 300 to 450 ml/½ to ¾ pint cheese sauce,
>   *see* page 143
> *For the soufflé topping:*
> 100 g/4 oz button or wild mushrooms
> 50 g/2 oz butter or margarine
> 25 g/1 oz flour
> 150 ml/¼ pint milk
> 3 eggs

Put the macaroni into at least 1.2 litres/2 pints well-seasoned boiling water and cook briskly until *al dente* (firm to the bite). Strain.

Make the sauce. Allow the smaller amount if you like a firm-textured macaroni cheese. Blend with the macaroni. Put this into a 1.8 litre/3 pint pie dish or good-sized casserole. Place in preheated oven, set to 180°C/350°F, Gas Mark 4 for 15 minutes while preparing the topping.

For the soufflé topping: Chop the mushrooms, heat the butter or margarine, add the mushrooms and cook for 5 minutes. Blend in the flour, then add the milk and stir as the mixture comes to the boil and becomes a thick sauce. Remove from the heat. Separate the eggs, beat the yolks in the mushroom sauce with seasoning to taste. Whisk the egg whites until just stiff, then fold into the other ingredients. Spoon over the hot macaroni cheese and continue baking for a further 30 minutes. Serve at once with a green salad. *Serves 6*

To make a change
Use cooked spinach or sorrel or chopped cooked peppers in the topping.
Tagliatelle with Mushrooms and Peppers: Toss the cooked pasta in a mixture of cooked button and wild mushrooms and sliced green, yellow and red peppers. Serve with Parmesan cheese.

Risotto Milanese

I love the texture of a good risotto, and *arborio* rice – often called medium grain, or Italian rice – gives a lovely creamy texture to the dish. Apart from choosing the right kind of rice, it is also important to add the liquid *gradually* to the rice during the cooking process. The following is a basic risotto, to which you can add other ingredients. The kind of stock used will vary according to the ingredients you want to add.

> 2 medium onions
> 1 garlic clove, optional
> 50 g/2 oz butter
> 2 tablespoons olive oil
> 300 to 350 g/10 to 12 oz *arborio* rice
> pinch saffron powder or few saffron strands,
>   optional, *see* method
> 1.2 to 1.5 litres/2 to 2½ pints chicken stock
> salt and freshly ground black pepper
> little white wine, optional

Peel and chop the onions and garlic. Heat half the butter and all the oil in a good-sized pan and add the onions and garlic. Cook for several minutes, then stir in the rice. Turn the grains in the onion mixture and heat gently until the rice turns golden. Add the saffron (if used) to the stock and heat. Pour enough hot stock over the rice to moisten it. Cook briskly for a short time, then add more stock. Season to taste. Continue adding hot stock as the rice cooks; it will take about 20 to 25 minutes and it should have a pleasantly moist consistency. Add the extra butter and wine towards the end of the cooking period.

Serve with plenty of grated Parmesan or other cheese.   *Serves 4 to 6*

To make a change
One of the most famous risottos is with chickens' livers; fry them with the onions then remove from the pan, so they are not over-cooked. Return to the pan towards the end of the cooking period. Bacon, sausages, fish and shellfish can be cooked separately and added at the last minute.
Vegetable Risottos: Add well-seasoned, cooked tomatoes, mushrooms of various kinds, sliced peppers, sliced courgettes and aubergines to the risotto towards the end of the cooking time.

Dolmas

Classic Dolmas are made with vine leaves but you can use cabbage leaves. Fillings are infinitely variable: try the Meatballs (page 116) or one of the Risotto mixtures (page 140) or use the vegetarian filling here.

> **12 to 16 vine leaves or 8 young cabbage leaves**
> **salt and freshly ground black pepper**
> *For the filling:*
> **2 medium onions**
> **2 garlic cloves**
> **4 medium tomatoes**
> **1 tablespoon olive oil**
> **175 g/6 oz cooked haricot or flageolet beans**
> **salt and freshly ground black pepper**
> **2 tablespoons chopped mixed herbs**
> *To cook the dolmas:*
> **600 m/1 pint vegetable stock**
> **2 tablespoons tomato purée (paste)**

Put the vine leaves or cabbage leaves in boiling, salted water for 2 minutes only. Boil steadily, drain and dry on kitchen paper. Spread flat. Peel and finely chop the onions and garlic. Skin and chop the tomatoes. Heat the oil, add these vegetables and cook for a few minutes, then add the beans, seasoning and herbs. Put some of the mixture on each leaf and fold these over the filling. Tie with fine cotton.. Put into a dish. Blend the stock and tomato purée with seasoning. Pour over the Dolmas. Cover the dish and cook for 1 hour in a preheated oven, set to 180°C/350°F, Gas Mark 4. The liquid can be thickened as described below if a sauce is required with the Dolmas.

To make a change
Vegetable Strudel: Prepare the filo pastry or strudel dough (*see* pages 155 and 156). Fill with a double amount of the mixture given in the recipe above and bake as Apple Strudel (*see* page 155).
Thickened Sauces and Gravies: Make a *beurre-manie* by blending 50 g/2 oz butter, margarine or other fat and 50 g/2 oz flour. Drop small amounts into the hot liquid above, or any stock. Whisk as it heats; continue until desired consistency is reached. *Beurre-manie* keeps well in the refrigerator.

141

Imam Bayeldi

This dish is so called because an Imam, an official of the mosque, fainted with delight when he tasted it. As some of the peel is removed from the aubergines, do not sprinkle with salt first.

> 4 medium aubergines
> 4 garlic cloves
> 6 tablespoons olive oil
> 675 g/1½ lb tomatoes, preferably plum type
> salt and freshly ground black pepper

Remove the ends from the aubergines. Cut the peel at regular intervals to give a striped effect. Make two slits in each aubergine. Peel and halve the garlic cloves; push one half into each slit. Heat the oil in a large, deep frying pan and cook the aubergines steadily, turning around from time to time, for 10 minutes. Remove from the pan. Chop the tomatoes (there is no need to skin them). Add them to the oil remaining in the frying pan; season well and simmer until they become a pulp. Add the aubergines and turn around in the tomato pulp. Cover the pan. Simmer for 10 to 15 minutes. Remove the garlic and serve hot or cold.

To make a change
Stuffed Aubergines: Score the skins of 2 large aubergines lightly, sprinkle with salt, leave for 30 minutes. The salt draws out the bitter taste from the skins. Rinse in cold water, dry and cut lengthways. Scoop out the centre pulp, chop this finely and add to your chosen stuffing. The filling for Dolmas (*see* page 141) is a very good one. If using it, cook the diced pulp with the onions, etc. Put the filling into the aubergine shells and top with wholemeal breadcrumbs and grated cheese. Bake for 40 minutes at 190°C/375°F, Gas Mark 5.
Stuffed Courgettes: Wipe large courgettes, but do not salt them. Proceed as aubergines, adding the selected stuffing. Baked halved courgettes are excellent topped with scrambled eggs, herbs and cheese.
To scramble eggs perfectly: Cook slowly in a saucepan, or top of a double saucepan, or steadily in a bowl in the microwave.

For each egg allow 15 g/½ oz butter and ½ to 1 tablespoon milk or single cream plus seasoning. Melt the butter, beat the eggs and milk or cream *lightly*, season, add to the butter and cook, stirring as little as possible. Serve at once.

Asparagus Cheese

Asparagus, like so many vegetables, is excellent with a cheese sauce or the Mornay sauce below. It turns the vegetable into a light main course. Always add the cheese *after the sauce has thickened*, and do not allow the sauce to boil rapidly afterwards or it will make the cheese stringy and tough. When buying asparagus make sure the stalks and heads are firm and green. Ar*y* sign of wrinkling means the vegetable is stale.

> **enough asparagus to serve 4**
> **salt and freshly ground black pepper**
> *For the cheese sauce:*
> **25 g/1 oz butter or margarine**
> **25 g/1 oz plain flour**
> **300 ml/½ pint milk, or** *see* **method**
> **100 g/4 oz Gruyere, Cheddar or other cheese**
> **1 teaspoon made English mustard or French**
> **mustard**

Cook the asparagus in salted water until tender. Drain and put into a heated serving dish. Make the sauce while cooking the asparagus, so that the asparagus does not have to be kept hot for any length of time.

Heat the butter or margarine in a pan, stir in the flour, then gradually blend in the milk. Bring to the boil and cook until thickened. This consistency is good for a *coating sauce*, but if you are adding foods to be cooked in the sauce as in Scampi Capriccio (*see* page 106) you need 450 ml/¾ pint of milk to allow for evaporation during cooking. Grate the cheese finely. Remove the pan from the heat, add the cheese, mustard and any seasoning required. Pour over the asparagus and serve at once.

To make a change
Mornay Sauce: This is based upon a béchamel rather than a white sauce as above. To make béchamel sauce, add a chopped onion and a little chopped celery to the milk. Bring this to the boil. Remove from the heat, cover, leave for an hour, then strain and use to make cheese sauce above.
Vegetable Pie: Cook a selection of seasonal vegetables, strain these and add to the sauce, made as above. Put into a pie dish. Top with creamed potatoes and grated cheese, or pastry, and bake until brown.
Eggs au Gratin: Hard-boil eggs, put into a flameproof dish, top with cheese sauce, breadcrumbs and grated cheese and brown under the grill.

143

Choux Pastry

You may be surprised to find this under savoury, rather than sweet, dishes; but choux pastry blends well with most foods. It is important to use *exactly* the correct proportions when making this pastry and to follow the various stages, which are italicized in the method, *very carefully.*

>
> **50 g/2 oz butter or margarine**
> **150 ml/¼ pint water**
> **65 g/2½ oz plain flour**
> **2 eggs – size 3**
>

Put the butter or margarine with the water into a saucepan. Heat until the fat has melted. *Remove from the heat* and stir in all the flour at once. Blend well, then return to a low heat and *stir until the mixture forms a firm ball.* Allow to cool. Whisk the eggs and beat gradually into the flour mixture. You may not need all the egg. The mixture should stand in soft peaks. Use to make various shapes, such as the Gougère below. Always *preheat* the oven before baking.

Vegetable Gougère

>
> **choux pastry, as above, and** *see* **method**
> *For the filling:*
> **cooked vegetables in cheese sauce,** *see* **page**
>   **143** *or*
> **filling as for Dolmas,** *see* **page 141**
>

Make the choux pastry, *see* above. For savoury choux you can add seasoning to the flour. For a deeper ring use 50 per cent more of each ingredient. Preheat the oven to 200°C/400°F, Gas Mark 6. Grease a flat baking tray or an ovenproof flan dish. Spoon or pipe the choux pastry into a ring shape. Bake the shallower ring for 30 minutes, and the deeper one for 35 to 40 minutes, or until well-risen and firm. Check this carefully. Make one or two slits in the pastry for the steam to escape. Add the hot filling just before serving. To serve the Gougère cold, add vegetables to a cheese-flavoured mayonnaise; the Dolmas filling is equally good hot or cold. Cool choux pastry *away from a draught.*

Cheese Cutlets

These cutlets are useful for packed meals, since they are good hot or cold.

> 175 g/6 oz Gruyère or Cheddar cheese
> 25 g/1 oz butter or margarine
> 25 g/1 oz flour
> 150 m/¼ pint milk
> salt and freshly ground black pepper
> 1 teaspoon made English mustard or French
>   mustard
> *To coat the cutlets:*
> 1 tablespoon flour
> 1 egg
> 50 g/2 oz crisp breadcrumbs
> *For frying:* oil

Grate the cheese finely. Heat the butter or margarine in a pan, stir in the flour, then blend in the milk and stir briskly as the stiff mixture (known as a *panada*) comes to the boil and thickens. Add the cheese, seasoning – including the mustard – and blend well. Allow to become sufficiently cold to form into 4 large or 8 small cutlet shapes.

Dust with seasoned flour. Beat the egg then brush the cutlets with this and coat in the crumbs. Pat these firmly into the sides of the cutlets. Chill for a short time if possible before frying. Heat a little oil in a frying pan and fry the cutlets on each side until crisp and golden brown. Drain on kitchen paper and serve hot or cold with vegetables or salad.

To make a change
Cheese and Vegetable Cutlets: Add 4 or 5 tablespoons of cooked peas and other diced, cooked vegetables. Choose other good cooking cheeses.
Bean Cutlets: Put cooked haricot, red kidney or flageolet beans into a food processor and make a thick purée. Use 300 ml/½ pint of this instead of the cheese mixture. You can add finely chopped fried onions, chopped savory (a herb that is ideal with beans) and other cooked, diced vegetables. Form into cutlet shapes and proceed as for Cheese Cutlets.
Egg Cutlets: Substitute 4 or 5 hard-boiled and chopped eggs for the cheese in the recipe above.

Mother's Salads

I am afraid it would be wrong to attribute some of these suggestions to my mother, since some ingredients, like beansprouts, were unknown to her, but she would have approved wholeheartedly of the various mixtures. I am not giving quantities, since the balance of ingredients in a salad is so much a matter of personal taste.

Where I mention lettuce, do look out for some interesting varieties: the changes of colour, texture and flavour enhance any salad.

Vinaigrette Dressing

All too often people write down proportions for a vinaigrette dressing as if they could never be altered. I find there are some occasions when I want to be more generous with the oil, others when I would rather use less. Choose extra virgin olive oil, for this is the best quality; but do not be afraid to use other oils occasionally if you want a lighter flavour, *see* page 89. Buy the best quality wine vinegar possible – it makes such a difference to the taste – or use lemon juice instead.

To make the dressing: Blend 1 teaspoon Dijon mustard with 3 tablespoons oil. Gradually blend in 1½ tablespoons wine vinegar and add seasoning to taste. You may like to add a good pinch of sugar.

Apple Salad: Dice dessert apples, blend with the dressing and chopped celery, finely chopped spring onions, chopped walnuts. Delicious with duck or cold pork.

Beetroot and Apple Salad: Blend equal quantities of diced dessert apples and cooked beetroot together. Add the dressing and lots of chopped chives and parsley.

Chinese Salad: Blend a few drops of soy sauce and sesame oil with the dressing. Shred Chinese leaves, top with raw beansprouts, sliced water chestnuts, canned or peeled and stoned fresh lychees and sesame seeds. Serve with Chinese meat or poultry dishes.

Currant Salad: Arrange small bunches of red and white currants on watercress and lettuce and top with dressing and nuts. Blackcurrants could be used instead, with sliced cucumber and tomatoes or pyramids of grated raw carrot. Currant salads are wonderful with poultry dishes.

Orange Salad: Arrange rings of orange and thin onion rings on a bed of lettuce; you can add rings of green and yellow pepper too.

More Salads

These salads are among those I have enjoyed in many parts of the world. They make an excellent start to a meal or a light main dish.

Green Bean Salad: Beans of all kinds make good, sustaining, salads. It is a good idea to cook extra haricots verts or French beans or sliced runner beans and serve these cold, topped with a little dressing and a generous amount of chopped parsley and chopped chives.

A more ambitious salad is made by blending cooked green beans with cooked or canned haricot beans or butter beans and red kidney beans. These give a pleasing blend of colours and textures. Always use plenty of chopped fresh herbs in the dressing, for beans need the 'bite' of these.

Moroccan Orange Salad: The recipe below is just one of the ways in which oranges are served in salads in Morocco. They are mixed with various vegetables or served with a dressing and plenty of olives.

This mixture of olives, tomatoes and green peppers looks as good as it tastes. Cut away the peel from 3 large oranges, slice the fruit into thin rings, remove any pips. Skin and thinly slice 3 or 4 large tomatoes. Deseed 2 green peppers and cut the pulp into very thin rings. Arrange these three ingredients in a neat design on flat plates. Make the Vinaigrette Dressing, as page 146, but add a little crushed garlic and a good pinch of paprika. Spoon over the salad. Chill well.

Mushroom and Avocado Salad: Choose small button mushrooms. Wipe these well but do not remove the skins. Peel, halve and stone the avocados. Cut the flesh into neat dice or wafer thin slices. Blend the mushrooms and avocados with Vinaigrette Dressing, made as page 146. Top the salad with chopped chives and finely diced red pepper.

Tomato and Mint Salad: Skin firm tomatoes and cut into wafer-thin slices. Arrange on a bed of mixed green salad. Top with a generous amount of thinly sliced spring onions and finely chopped mint. Moisten with a little Vinaigrette Dressing, made as page 146, to which you can add a pinch of chilli powder or a few drops of tabasco sauce.

Waldorf Salad: There are many versions of this refreshing American fruit salad. I like to mix equal amounts of neatly diced celery, diced unpeeled dessert apples and halved deseeded grapes. These ingredients are blended with mayonnaise, or a mixture of mayonnaise and a well-seasoned yoghurt. Top with a generous amount of coarsely chopped pecan nuts or walnuts. Diced melon could be added, or used instead of the grapes.

147

Sweet Potato and Apple Bake

Now that sweet potatoes and yams are regularly on sale in this country, we can use them in place of ordinary potatoes. The first recipe is one I learned in South Africa from a wonderfully inventive cook.

> **900 g/2 lb sweet potatoes**
> **2 large crisp dessert apples (eg Granny Smiths)**
> **50 g/2 oz butter**
> **4 tablespoons brown sugar or honey**
> **2 tablespoons orange juice or sherry**
> **pinch salt**

Scrub the sweet potatoes and cook them in their jackets in a little boiling water until almost tender, or bake in a microwave. Remove the core from the apples but do not skin them; cut into rings. Skin the sweet potatoes. Melt the butter and blend with the sugar or honey, the orange juice or sherry, and salt. Arrange the sweet potatoes, apples and the sugar or honey mixture in layers in a deep casserole. End with a layer of sweet potatoes and a little of the sweet mixture. Cover the casserole and bake in a preheated oven set to 160°C/325°F, Gas Mark 3 for 30 to 35 minutes, until the potatoes and apples are piping hot and tender.

This particular dish is excellent with game. You can reduce the amount of sweetening by half without spoiling the flavour.   ***Serves 6 to 8***

To make a change
Use sliced canned or fresh pineapple instead of apples.

Yam and Potato Bake

Peel and thinly slice 450 g/1 lb yams and 450 g/1 lb ordinary potatoes. Heat 300 ml/½ pint milk with 50 g/2 oz butter or margarine and a generous amount of salt and pepper.

Arrange the potatoes and yams in neat layers in an ovenproof serving dish (an oblong shape is easier to pack). Pour the hot milk mixture over the vegetables. Do not cover the dish. Bake for 1 to 1¼ hours, or until tender and golden brown on top, in a preheated oven set to 160°C/325°F, Gas Mark 3.   ***Serves 6 to 8***

Lentil and Bean Stir-Fry

Stir-frying is an ideal way of cooking young vegetables. This dish is very satisfying and nutritious and gives a good blending of flavours and colours. It is important to cook the haricot beans for just a few minutes in boiling water before stir-frying. The lentils must be cooked until just tender.

225 g/8 oz haricot verts
100 g/4 oz lentils, preferably the green type
salt and freshly ground black pepper
2 bunches of spring onions
175 g/6 oz small button mushrooms
1 red pepper
1 green pepper
2 tablespoons sunflower oil
1 teaspoon cornflour
150 ml/¼ pint vegetable stock
1 tablespoon light soy sauce
pinch chilli powder (optional)
2 tablespoons rice wine or dry sherry
100 g/4 oz beansprouts

Remove the ends of the haricot beans. Put into boiling water and cook for 3 or 4 minutes only, then strain and put on one side. Put the lentils in cold water to cover with salt and pepper to taste. Bring the water to boiling point, cover the pan and cook for about 20 minutes, or until the lentils are just tender. Drain well.

Cut the tops from the spring onions. Chop a little of the green stems to use as a garnish. Wipe the mushrooms and leave whole. Halve the peppers, remove the cores and seeds and cut the pulp into thin strips. Heat the oil in a wok or deep frying pan. Put in the spring onions, mushrooms, haricot beans and stir-fry for 3 minutes. Add the peppers and continue cooking, stirring all the time, for another 3 minutes. Add the lentils and heat with the other ingredients for 1 or 2 minutes.

Blend the cornflour with the stock, soy sauce and chilli powder. Pour over the ingredients in the pan. Stir until slightly thickened. Add the rice wine or sherry and the beansprouts and cook for 2 minutes. Top with the chopped green stems from the spring onions. Serve with cooked rice.

DESSERTS

The desserts in this section reflect some of the more interesting recipes I have made and enjoyed during my career. All of them are delicious. Some, like the sorbets and ice creams, are fairly rich, as they contain a good proportion of cream. The recipes indicate when the cream can be replaced by yoghurt or fromage frais.

The recipe below dates from the War years, when rationing made it extremely difficult to make desserts. Most people did try to include a dessert course, however, for it made meals more appetising and satisfying.

Czech Plum Dumplings

These small, fruit-filled dumplings were a great treat during the War. We had no cream or curd cheese, so used grated scraps of cheese and moistened these with milk. The pastry included a little potato, to save using so much fat. It is an exceptionally light pastry.

For the pastry:
75 g/3 oz cooked potatoes
150 g/5 oz self-raising flour
pinch salt
75 g/3 oz margarine
water to bind
For the filling:
about 12 ripe plums
150 g/5 oz cream cheese or curd cheese

Sieve or mash the potatoes until smooth, sift the flour and salt; rub in the margarine. Add the potatoes and enough water to make a soft rolling consistency. It should leave your fingers very slightly sticky. Halve and stone the plums; sandwich the two halves together with the cheese. Divide the pastry into portions and roll around the plums with floured fingers. Drop into a pan of rapidly boiling water and cook for 20 minutes. Serve with sugar, cream or ice cream or custard. (*See also* page 155.) Slices of apple and cheese could be used instead of plums.

Pancakes

There is nothing difficult about making this basic pancake batter. What can be a problem though, is producing beautifully wafer-thin, and golden pancakes that do *not* stick to the pan. Many people make the mistake of using oil or fat when cooking each pancake. If you have a really well-behaved pan, you can manage without any fat at all. Even if your pan is less than perfect, you should be 100 per cent successful if you use a very little oil for the first pancake *only,* and add oil or butter to the batter.

> **110 g/4 oz plain flour**
> **pinch salt**
> **2 eggs – size 1 or 2**
> **275 ml/9 fl oz milk, or milk and water**
> **1 tablespoon oil or melted butter**

Sift the flour and salt into a bowl, add the eggs one by one and beat until smooth. Gradually incorporate the milk, or milk and water.

Whisk the batter well immediately before cooking. Add the oil or butter. Rub the base of the pan with a few drops of oil, heat well then pour in just enough batter to give a wafer-thin coating. Cook steadily for 2 minutes, or until the pancake moves freely in the pan, then turn or toss and cook on the second side. Continue like this until all the batter is used. Keep hot on a dish over boiling water. ***Makes about 12***

***Fillings for pancakes*:** There are so many different ways to fill pancakes. Traditionally in Britain we roll the pancakes on sugared paper and serve them with lemon, but why not be adventurous and try filling the pancakes with cooked fruit, or jam and cottage cheese or really firm ice cream? Pancakes for a special occasion can be filled with thick apricot, or other fruit purée, then rolled or folded and topped with a spoonful of Brandy Butter, *see* recipe below.

Brandy Butter*:** Cream together 100 g/4 oz unsalted butter with 175 g/6 oz sifted icing sugar. Gradually add 2 to 4 tablespoons brandy. Chill very well before serving. This is known also as *hard sauce.* The butter mixture can be flavoured with a little finely grated orange zest and Curaçao can be used instead of brandy. ***Serves 6

Christmas Pudding – 1954

This recipe is based upon the Christmas Pudding I showed on BBC TV in 1954, the year that rationing ended. It has a delicious and subtle flavour, due to the diversity of ingredients used. I use butter as the fat, for I find this makes a better-flavoured pudding than the traditional suet. You can substitute vegetarian margarine for the butter.

110 g/4 oz butter
50 g/2 oz prunes, weight without stones
50 g/2 oz dried apricots
110 g/4 oz candied peel
110 g/4 oz blanched almonds
50 g/2 oz glacé cherries
50 g/2 oz apple (weight when finely grated)
50 g/2 oz raw carrot (weight when finely grated)
450 g/1 lb dried fruit, preferably:
  225 g/8 oz seedless raisins
  110 g/4 oz currants
  110 g/4 oz sultanas
finely grated zest and juice of ½ lemon
finely grated zest and juice of ½ small orange
50 g/2 oz plain flour
110 g/4 oz fine soft breadcrumbs
110 g/4 oz moist brown sugar
½ teaspoon freshly grated nutmeg
½ teaspoon ground cinnamon
½ teaspoon mixed spice
2 eggs – size 1 or 2
150 ml/¼ pint ale or dark beer

Melt the butter; cut the prunes, apricots, candied peel, almonds and cherries into small pieces. Mix with all the other ingredients. Stir well to blend, then cover and leave overnight. Put into one 1.5 to 1.8 litre/2½ to 3 pint greased pudding basin. Cover well and steam over boiling water for at least 5 hours. Remove the damp covering and put on a dry layer. Store in a cool, dry place. On Christmas Day steam the pudding again for 2 hours.

Serve with Brandy Butter, recipe on page 151. **Serves 8 to 10**

Pecan Pie

Walnuts or hazelnuts can be used instead of pecans if you prefer.

For the pastry:
175 g/6 oz plain flour
pinch salt
85 g/3 oz butter or margarine
1 tablespoon caster sugar
water to bind
For the filling:
110 to 175 g/4 to 6 oz pecan nuts
50 g/2 oz butter
3 eggs – size 1 or 2
110 g/4 oz soft light brown sugar
½ teaspoon vanilla essence
5 level tablespoons golden (corn) syrup

Sift the flour and salt into a basin, rub in the butter or margarine until it looks like fine breadcrumbs, add the sugar and enough water to make a firm rolling consistency. Wrap the pastry and chill for a short time then roll out and line a 20 to 23 cm/8 to 9-inch flan tin or dish. Put greaseproof paper or foil into the flan shape and top with crusts of bread or plastic baking beans. Chill again if possible, as this helps the pastry keep its shape. Preheat the oven to 220°C/425°F, Gas Mark 7. Bake the pie shape for 7 minutes only, then remove the paper or foil. Allow to cool. Chop the nuts quite coarsely, melt the butter and mix with the nuts. Whisk the eggs and sugar until thick.

Blend with the butter and nuts, stir in the essence and syrup. Spoon into the pastry case. Lower the oven heat to 160°C/325°F, Gas Mark 3. Bake for 30 minutes, or until firm. Serve warm or cold.   *Serves 4 to 6*

To make a change
Coconut Cream Pie: Make the pastry case and bake for 7 minutes as above. Whisk 3 eggs – size 1 or 2 – with 50 g/2 oz soft brown sugar, add ½ teaspoon vanilla essence, 150 ml/¼ pint single cream and 110 g/4 oz desiccated coconut. Lower the oven heat to 150°C/300°F, Gas Mark 2. Spoon the filling into the pastry. Bake for 40 minutes or until just firm. Serve hot or cold.

Strawberry Shortcake

The shortcake can be made throughout the year, and sandwiched together with different fruits, depending what is in season. The coulis – the name given to sweet or savoury sauces that are not thickened with flour – blends well with the shortcake, or other desserts. This recipe produces a light-textured and economical shortcake. Serve when fresh.

For the shortcake mixture:
85 g/3 oz butter or margarine
225 g/8 oz self-raising flour
110 g/4 oz caster sugar
1 egg - size 1 or 2
milk to bind
For the filling:
450 g/1 lb strawberries
sugar to taste
little butter

Preheat the oven to 220°C/425°F, Gas Mark 7. Lightly grease a large baking tray. Rub the butter or margarine into the flour, add the sugar. Beat the egg, add to the flour mixture with sufficient milk to make a soft rolling consistency. Roll, or pat out, the dough until 0.5 cm/¼ inch in thickness and cut into 8 to 12 rounds for smaller individual shortcakes. If making one large shortcake, divide the dough into equal halves and form each into a 20 cm/8 inch rounds. Place on the baking tray. Bake small shortcakes for about 10 minutes and larger ones for 15 to 20 minutes, or until well risen, firm and brown.

Slice most of the strawberries and add sugar to taste. Save a few whole berries for decoration. When the shortcakes are cool, sandwich together with a little butter and the sliced strawberries. Top with the whole fruit. Serve when fresh with cream or yoghurt or fromage frais.   *Serves 4 to 6*

To make a change
Omit the butter when sandwiching the shortcakes together; use sliced strawberries only, top with whipped cream, and serve with this coulis.
Strawberry Coulis: Heat 50 g/2 oz caster sugar with 1 tablespoon lemon juice and 1 tablespoon water until dissolved. Sieve or liquidize 450 g/1 lb of strawberries. Blend with the syrup. Serve cold or heat for a short time. Do not overcook or you will lose the fresh fruit flavour.

Apple Strudel

Now that filo (phyllo) pastry is available, it is much easier to make this famous dessert. If you would like to make the authentic strudel pastry, the recipe is on page 156.

For the filling:
50 g/2 oz butter
50 g/2 oz soft breadcrumbs
50 g/2 oz soft brown or caster sugar
675 g/1½ lb cooking apples (weight when
  peeled and cored)
75 g/3 oz raisins or sultanas
1 teaspoon finely grated lemon zest
½ teaspoon ground cinnamon
For the covering:
filo pastry, *see* method
50 g/2 oz butter or margarine
little icing sugar

Heat the butter for the filling and add the breadcrumbs. Fry until evenly crisp and brown. Allow to cool, then add the sugar. Slice the apples very thinly, blend with the crumbs and remaining filling ingredients.

The size of filo pastry sheets varies but you will need approximately 12 sheets to fit into a tin about 24 x 20 cm/10 x 8 inches. If you have to cut the pastry and have some half-sheets left over, use these for middle layers, not for the bottom or top layers. Unwrap the sheets of pastry one at a time. (Keep the rest covered until required, so they do not dry.)

Melt the butter or margarine. Place the first sheet of filo pastry on the tin and brush with a little melted fat. Add the next sheet, brush with fat. Continue until 6 sheets have been used. Add the filling; spread evenly over the pastry base. Top with the rest of the pastry, brushing each layer with fat. Brush top with the last of the melted fat. Press edges together.

Preheat the oven to 200°C/400°F, Gas Mark 6. Bake for 40 minutes. Reduce the heat slightly after 20 minutes, or when the pastry is becoming brown. You need adequate cooking time to soften the apples. Top the strudel with sifted icing sugar just before serving. It is equally good served hot or cold.

Makes 8 slices

There are other sweet strudels on page 156 and a savoury strudel on page 141.

Strudel Dough

This is the dough I use for a strudel, instead of ready-made filo pastry. Give yourself plenty of time to roll and stretch the dough, for it must be paper thin. This is more pliable than filo pastry, so it can be rolled with the filling inside when making a strudel.

> 150 g/5 oz strong flour (type used for bread-
>   making) or plain flour
> pinch salt
> 1½ tablespoons melted butter or olive oil
> 1 egg yolk
> warm water to bind

Sift the flour and salt into a bowl, add 1 tablespoon of the melted butter or oil, the egg yolk, then sufficient water to make a firm dough. Knead until smooth. Return to the bowl, top with the remaining butter or oil, cover and leave for 30 minutes. Then knead again.

Spread a large cloth over the table, flour this lightly then roll and pull the dough until very thin. Add the apple filling, recipe as on page 155, roll and form into a horseshoe shape on the baking tray. Brush with a little butter and bake as page 155. Brush with butter during the baking process.

To make a change
Plum or Cherry Strudels: Use halved plums or stoned Morello, or black dessert cherries instead of apples in the filling on page155 and filo pastry or the strudel dough above. Bake as page 155.
Plum Purses: Use filo pastry or the dough above (filo pastry is more suitable for this purpose). Cut out squares, each sufficiently large to envelop large dessert plums. Use 2 or 3 layers of filo pastry, placed on top of each another. Brush each layer with melted butter or margarine. If using strudel dough, use one layer only. Halve large dessert plums, carefully remove the stones and fill the centres with cream or curd cheese. Press the halves together again, place in the centre of the pastry squares. Bring the edges together at the top, rather like a fluted purse. Brush with melted butter or margarine and bake for 20 to 25 minutes in a preheated oven, set to 220°C/425°F, Gas Mark 7. Dust with caster sugar and serve hot.

Brazilian Cream

This is a very luxurious version of a baked custard. The mixture of caramel, chocolate and coffee flavours give a pudding that is unusual and absolutely delicious.

75 g/3 oz caster or granulated sugar
4 tablespoons water
300 ml/½ pint milk
110 g/4 oz plain chocolate
1 tablespoon instant coffee powder
4 eggs – size 1 or 2
2 egg yolks
450 ml/¾ pint single cream
few drops vanilla essence
extra sugar if desired
To decorate the dessert:
50 g/2 oz Brazil nuts
small amount of plain chocolate
little Demerara sugar
150 ml/¼ pint double cream, optional

For the caramel: Put the sugar with 3 tablespoons of the water into a strong saucepan, stir until the sugar has dissolved, then boil steadily without stirring, until a golden-brown caramel. Add the other tablespoon of cold water immediately to cool the mixture slightly. Leave in the pan until cold, then add the milk. Return to a gentle heat and stir until the caramel and milk are blended together. *Do not* allow to boil, or the mixture will curdle. Add the chocolate and coffee and heat gently until dissolved.

Whisk the eggs and egg yolks with the cream and vanilla essence, pour on the mixture from the pan. Taste this and add a little sugar if desired. Strain into a 1.2 to 1.5 litre/2 to 2½ pint dish and stand in a tin of cold water (the water should come half-way up the pudding dish). Bake for 1¾ to 2 hours, until firm, in a preheated oven, set to 140 to 150°C/275 to 300°F, Gas Mark 1 to 2.

Allow to become cold. Chop most of the nuts, saving just one or two. Grate the chocolate. Sprinkle the nuts, chocolate and sugar on top of the dessert. Whip the cream until it stands in peaks, spoon or pipe around the edge of the dish. Add the whole nut(s).   *Serves 6*

Crème Brûlée

This delicious sweet is simply a well-chilled creamy egg custard, topped with sugar and grilled until the sugar becomes brown and crisp. An egg custard is richer in flavour if you use a higher proportion of egg yolks than egg whites. It is essential that the custard is cooked gently so it never boils. Even at a low setting, care must be taken that it does not cook for too long a period. If it does, the mixture will eventually reach a high enough temperature to curdle (separate).

> **3 eggs – size 1 or 2**
> **2 egg yolks**
> **40 g/1½ oz caster sugar**
> **450 ml/¾ pint milk and 150 ml/¼ pint single**
>   **cream or use all milk**
> **little vanilla essence or use a vanilla pod**
> *For the topping:*
> **75 g/3 oz Demerara sugar**

Beat the eggs and egg yolks with the sugar. Warm, but do not boil, the milk and cream, or milk, with the vanilla essence or with the vanilla pod. Pour the liquid on to the beaten eggs then strain into the cooking container. Cook the custard over hot, but not boiling, water until the mixture thickly coats the back of a wooden spoon. Stir or whisk continually during the cooking process. Follow the manufacturer's recommendations if using the microwave and whisk every few seconds. When the custard is cooked, transfer to individual dishes or one large flameproof dish suitable for putting under a heated grill. Remove the vanilla pod at this stage, rinse in cold water and dry.

Chill the custard. Just before serving, top with the Demerara sugar and place under the grill, set to moderate. Heat until the topping is hot, brown and crisp. Serve at once or allow to become cold.

To make a change
Caramel Brûlée: Make the caramel as in Brazilian Cream (*see* page 157); add the milk and cream as in the recipe above. Heat gently until blended, then pour on to the beaten eggs, as in the recipe above. Add sugar to taste. Bake as Brazilian Cream until firm. Top with blanched almonds and sugar and brown under the grill, as described above.

Almond Rice Pudding

I created this recipe from Norwegian Christmas Porridge, in which one solitary almond is hidden in a rich rice pudding. The boy or girl who finds this in their portion will be the first in the family to marry.

75 g/3 oz short grain (pudding) rice
600 ml/1 pint milk
25 g/1 oz butter
few drops almond essence
50 g/2 oz caster sugar
100 g/4 oz blanched almonds
50 g/2 oz glacé cherries
50 g/2 oz candied peel
150 ml/¼ pint double cream

Preheat the oven to 140°C/275°F, Gas Mark 1. Grease a 1.2 litre/2 pint pie dish. Put the rice, milk, butter, essence and sugar into a saucepan. Bring the milk to boiling point, stir well then pour the ingredients into the pie dish. Bake for 1½ hours and remove the pudding from the oven.

Chop the almonds, cherries and peel. Stir half into the pudding with the cream. Return to the oven for another 1½ hours, or until the rice is tender. Top with the remaining nuts, cherries and peel and serve.

To make a change
Omit the cherries and peel in the recipe above. Use the almonds only and serve with the cherry jam below.

Black Cherry Jam: Not all fruits require the same amount of sugar in jam-making. Some fruits, such as blackcurrants and redcurrants are very rich in pectin and you should use *less* fruit than sugar. Where fruits are lacking in natural pectin, such as ripe cherries or strawberries, you have a jam that sets better if you use *more* fruit than sugar, as in this recipe. Always use ripe black cherries.

Stone the cherries and, after stoning, weigh the fruit. Allow only 400 g/14 oz sugar plus 1 tablespoon lemon juice to each 450 g/1 lb cherries. Put the cherries, sugar and any juice from the cherries when stoning into a pan, stir until the sugar has dissolved. Boil without stirring, until setting point is reached. Cool slightly, stir to distribute the cherries, then spoon into heated jars and cover. **Makes 675 g/1½ lb**

Baked Bananas

I first started to bake bananas in the late 1940s. Fresh bananas were still scarce, but dried bananas were delicious. Here are recipes for both.

25 g/1 oz butter
50 g/2 oz soft brown sugar
1 teaspoon finely grated orange zest
1 tablespoon lemon juice
150 ml/¼ pint orange juice
8 small bananas
1 tablespoon rum or brandy

Preheat the oven to 180°C/350°F, Gas Mark 4. Put the butter and sugar into a shallow casserole and heat for 5 minutes, add the orange zest and fruit juices and return to the oven for a further 5 minutes. Peel the bananas and put into the mixture. Turn around so they are well coated then bake for 15 minutes. Add the rum or brandy just before serving.

To make a change

Stuffed Baked Bananas: Split 8 bananas lengthways. Blend 3 tablespoons orange marmalade and 25 g/1 oz desiccated coconut. Sandwich the bananas with this mixture. Use only 25 g/1 oz sugar in the sauce above.

Baked Dried Bananas: Melt the butter with just 25 g/1 oz sugar, add the fruit zest and fruit juices. Soak 8 halved dried bananas in this mixture for 1 hour, then bake as above.

Figs in Ouzo

The joy of this dessert is its simplicity. Ouzo is the clear spirit drunk in Greece and neighbouring countries. It has a strong aniseed flavour.

Allow 2 or 3 fresh figs per person and cover these with ouzo, or ouzo mixed with white wine. Chill for several hours before serving.

To make a change

Substitute rum plus white wine for the ouzo, if preferred.

Skinned and halved fresh peaches can be served in the same way or baked as in Baked Bananas above.

Chinese Toffee Apples

These apples and the Moroccan pastries, B'stillas, below, make original desserts. There is a do-it-yourself element for your dinner guests in creating the toffee effect in these apple slices, as explained in the recipe.

4 large dessert apples or small cooking apples
1 egg – size 1 or 2
3 level tablespoons flour
For the toffee syrup:
110 g/4 oz caster or granulated sugar
2 teaspoons sunflower oil
2 tablespoons water
3 tablespoons thin honey or golden (corn) syrup
For frying: oil

Peel and core the apples and cut into slices 1.5 cm/$\frac{1}{2}$ inch thick. Beat the egg. Coat the apple slices with the egg and then with the flour.

To make the syrup: Heat the sugar and oil together, stir until the sugar has dissolved then boil steadily, without stirring, until golden brown, add the water and honey or golden syrup; heat until dissolved.

Bring the oil for frying the apples to 180°C/350°F – or until a cube of day-old bread turns golden in 50 seconds. Add the apple slices and fry for 3 to 4 minutes, or until golden-brown and crisp. Drain on kitchen paper then drop into the hot syrup. Coat the apple slices in the syrup. Carry the pan with the hot syrup and apples to the table.

Give each person a small bowl containing cold water and ice cubes; you take apple slices with chopsticks from the hot syrup and plunge these into the iced water. The coating sets as a crisp toffee.

Sweet B'stillas

Cut small rounds of filo pastry or strudel dough, see pages 155 and 156. Both are similar to Moroccan *warkha* pastry. Have two layers of filo pastry, or one of strudel dough. Brush with plenty of butter. Top with ground almonds, sugar and a little ground cinnamon. Moisten the edges and fold over to enclose the filling. Bake in a preheated oven, set to 220°C/425°F, Gas Mark 7 for 15 to 20 minutes. Dust with sugar.

Maraschino and Apricot Mousse

This recipe makes a delicious jellied dessert. I find it easier and more satisfactory to soften gelatine in cold liquid before dissolving it in the microwave or over hot water. Do *not* overheat the gelatine.

> 450 ml/³⁄₄ pint smooth apricot purée, *see* method
> 1 x 11 g sachet, or 1 level tablespoon, gelatine
> 2 tablespoons water
> 2 eggs – size 1 or 2
> 50 g/2 oz caster sugar
> 300 ml/½ pint double cream or thick yoghurt
> 4 tablespoons Maraschino cherries

The apricot purée can be made by cooking dried or fresh apricots, or by using canned fruit. Liquidize 225 g/8 oz cooked dried apricots or 450 g/1 lb stoned cooked or canned fruit. Add enough syrup from the fruit to give just 450 ml/³⁄₄ pint. The purée must be thick.

Sprinkle the gelatine on to the cold water; stand for 2 minutes to soften. Dissolve in the microwave cooker or over a pan of hot, but not boiling, water. Add 4 tablespoons of the apricot purée to the dissolved gelatine; return to the heat for 1 minute. Mix with the rest of the purée. Separate the eggs and beat the yolks and sugar until thick and creamy. Whip the cream until it just stands in peaks. Blend the egg yolk mixture and three-quarters of the cream, or yoghurt, with the apricot jelly. Finally, whisk the egg whites until stiff, fold into the mixture.

Chill until beginning to set. Chop the cherries and fold most of these into the apricot mousse. Spoon into individual glasses. When set, top with the remaining cream or yoghurt and the cherries   *Serves 6*

To make a change
Rhubarb Mousse: Cook enough rhubarb, with sugar to taste, to produce 450 ml/³⁄₄ pint purée. Do not add liquid, since rhubarb contains such a high percentage of water. You can add the finely grated zest of 1 or 2 oranges when cooking the fruit and soften the gelatine in orange juice instead of water. Add blanched (skinned) pistachio nuts to the mixture instead of cherries.

Maraschino and Raspberry Coulis: Omit the cherries from the Apricot Mousse. Top the dessert with a coulis made by blending sieved raspberries with Maraschino liqueur and sugar to taste.

Orange Syllabub

A syllabub is a clever mixture of cream, or an alternative, and alcohol. Syllabubs made several centuries ago were so liquid in consistency that they were more like a drink than a dessert.

The ideal syllabub should be a soft, delicate texture and well chilled.

> **3 large oranges**
> **75 g/3 oz loaf sugar,** *see* **method**
> **150 ml/¼ pint white wine**
> **450 ml/¾ pint double or whipping cream,** *see*
>   **method for alternatives**
> **2 tablespoons Curaçao**

Wash the oranges in very hot water, then dry them well. This is necessary these days since many citrus fruits are coated with a thin film of wax to protect the fruit and add to their keeping qualities.

Rub the lumps of sugar over the outside of the oranges, so that the sugar absorbs the oil and the very top zest. Put the flavoured sugar into a bowl, crush with a fork and then add the wine. Halve 2 of the oranges and squeeze out 4 tablespoons of the juice. Cut the segments from the third orange and put on one side for decoration.

Whip the cream until it stands in peaks. Whipping cream contains less fat and produces a greater volume than double cream, but is never quite as stiff. You can use thick yoghurt or fromage frais for a less high-caloried dessert. Fold the cream, or alternative, into the orange mixture together with the Curaçao. Chill well, then gently stir and spoon into chilled glasses or dishes. Top with the orange segments.

Serve with sweet biscuits. *Serves 6 to 8*

To make a change
Instead of adding orange juice to the mixture, add small pieces of the orange segments.
Frosted Syllabub: The mixture above does not freeze well, because of its high liquid content, but it can be frozen until it is just like melting ice.
Lemon Syllabub: Use 2 lemons instead of oranges, plus a little more sugar. Clementines or grapefruit can be used instead.
Raspberry Syllabub: Use crushed or whole raspberries instead of oranges. A squeeze of lemon juice helps the flavour.

Citrus Sorbets

A sorbet is a light and delicate frozen mixture, based upon fruit or fruit juices. The American sherberts are similar to sorbets, but purists insist that a true sherbert should contain egg whites or a little cream; whereas these ingredients are not essential for a sorbet.

Sorbets can be served between courses, at the start of a meal, or as a dessert. Ice-cream makers are wonderful for sorbets, for they aerate the mixture during freezing. You can whisk the mixture, or incorporate egg whites, to achieve a similar effect.

This recipe is a good basic one to follow when using fruit juice. Instead of the mixture of flavours suggested, you could choose any fruits that have a high juice content, such as apples, grapefruit, orange, passion fruit, pineapple, pomegranate, etc. When the fruit flavour is very intense, such as in lemon, dilute with more water, or use white or rosé wine to add a piquant taste.

Adjust the amount of sugar according to the fruit and be clever with additional ingredients; try adding one or two scented geranium leaves, or sprigs of lemon balm, or a pinch of ground ginger, to add flavour.

> **150 ml/¼ pint water**
> **strips of citrus fruit zest**
> **150 to 175 g/5 to 6 oz caster sugar, or according**
> **to personal taste**
> **600 ml/1 pint mixed citrus fruit juices**
> **2 egg whites, optional**

Heat the water and fruit zest gently for 5 minutes. Add the sugar and stir until dissolved. Strain and cool. Blend with the fruit juice. Freeze until mushy. Whisk the egg whites until stiff, fold into the mixture, then continue freezing. Omit the egg whites if the mixture lacks a strong flavour, for they will dilute the taste. Remove from the freezer for 20 minutes before serving, to give the right texture.   ***Serves 6***

To make a change
Mango Sorbet: This is a good example of using fruit purées to make sorbets. There is no need to make a sugar syrup. Simply flavour the fresh fruit purée with sugar to taste. You may like to add a little lemon juice. Freeze until mushy and then beat hard. To make a lighter mixture, fold in the whisked egg whites half way through freezing.

Vanilla Ice Cream

There are many ways of making ice cream, and two basic recipes are given on this page. One of the best uses whisked eggs and cream. If you have an ice-cream maker, you can choose less rich mixtures, but when using an ordinary freezer, you *must* include a higher percentage of fat. If you substitute yoghurt for some of the cream it must be full-fat yoghurt. The second recipe omits eggs and should be used by anyone wary of using uncooked eggs because of health warnings.

> **2 eggs – size 1 or 2**
> **½ teaspoon vanilla essence**
> **50 g/2 oz icing sugar**
> **300 ml/½ pint double or whipping cream**

Put the eggs and vanilla into a mixing bowl, and sift in the icing sugar. Whisk until thick and creamy – you should be able to see the trail of the whisk. Whip the cream until it stands in peaks and fold into the egg mixture. Freeze until firm. This recipe does not require beating.

To make a change

Vanilla Ice Cream No.2: Blend 1 level tablespoon of cornflour with 150 ml/¼ pint milk, 150 ml/¼ pint single cream, 50 g/2 oz sugar and ¼ teaspoon vanilla essence. Heat, stirring well. When thickened, cool and freeze until mushy. Beat and blend with 300 ml/½ pint whipped cream.

Caramel Ice Cream: Make a caramel with 75 g/3 oz sugar and 3 tablespoons water, as described on page 157. Allow to cool. Add 4 tablespoons milk or single cream. Heat, without boiling, until the caramel has blended with the milk or cream. Allow to cool then blend with either of the Vanilla Ice Cream mixtures.

Chocolate Ice Cream: Melt 110 to 175 g/4 to 6 oz plain chocolate, allow to cool and blend with either of the Vanilla Ice Cream mixtures. You can use 50 to 75 g/2 to 3 oz chocolate powder instead.

Coffee Ice Cream: Use 1½ to 2 level tablespoons instant coffee powder and dilute with 2 tablespoons hot water, cool and add to either of the Vanilla Ice Cream mixtures. Increase the amount of sugar to 75 g/3 oz.

Strawberry Ice Cream: Make 300 ml/½ pint fresh strawberry purée. Freeze until slightly mushy, then blend with the rest of the ingredients in either Vanilla Ice Cream mixture. Omit the vanilla essence; increase the sugar to 75 g/3 oz. You can also use other fruits.

Pistachio Mallow

Marshmallows are an excellent ingredient in ice cream, particularly if you do not want to use uncooked eggs or egg whites. Marshmallows contain egg whites and gelatine and both ingredients are extremely valuable in giving a good texture to the mixture. The egg whites used in confectionery are dried and considered 100 per cent safe.

Marshmallows do not affect the texture or flavour of the ice cream. The pink ones can change the colour, so select white ones for a vanilla ice cream or where you want the colour to be pale.

Do not overheat the marshmallows: use the DEFROST setting of a microwave or melt over hot, not boiling, water. When the marshmallows are nearly melted, remove from the heat – they continue melting in the warm bowl. In the first recipe the marshmallows are melted completely. In Marshmallow Medley small pieces are left in the mixture.

> **175 g/6 oz white marshmallows**
> **150 ml/¼ pint white wine or milk**
> **300 ml/½ pint double or whipping cream**
> **175 g/6 oz pistachio nuts**
> **icing sugar to taste,** *see* **method**

Cut the marshmallows into quarters with damp kitchen scissors; this helps them to melt evenly. Put into a bowl with the white wine or milk and melt in the microwave or over hot water, *see* above. Allow to become quite cool and stiffen slightly again. Whip the cream until it stands in peaks and fold into the marshmallow mixture. Skin the pistachio nuts. To do this put them into boiling water for a few seconds. Remove from the water, cool slightly and then pull away the skins. Dry on kitchen paper and chop finely. Blend with the other ingredients. Add icing sugar if desired.

To make a change
Use the basic mixture above, without the nuts, instead of the Ice Cream recipes on page 165. The liquid in which the marshmallows are melted can be fruit purée or fruit juice or various kinds of wine.
Marshmallow Medley: Follow the proportions in the recipe above, but use pink and white marshmallows and half melt these. When cold, fold in the whipped cream with 175 g/6 oz chopped canned pineapple, 110 g/4 oz chopped Maraschino cherries, 100 g/4 oz chopped nuts and sugar to taste.

SCONES – TEABREADS – BISCUITS – CAKES

To ensure success when baking, always use the exact amount of basic ingredients given in the recipe. You might spoil the result if you use more fat or syrup, or fewer eggs than stated.

Always preheat the oven to the setting given. The cooking time has been checked carefully, but remember, ovens vary slightly, so test whether your cake or scones are cooked, as mentioned in the recipes. The size of the cake tin is given where this is important. This plays a part in determining the cooking time. If you do not possess exactly the right size and use a slightly larger cake tin the cooking time will be a few minutes shorter, because you have less depth of mixture. If you use a smaller tin the cooking time will be slightly longer because you have a greater depth of mixture. You may, therefore, need to lower the oven heat slightly near the end of the cooking time, to prevent the cake becoming over-brown.

Self-raising flour is given in recipes where appropriate. You can use plain flour plus baking powder instead. Allow 2 level teaspoons to each 225 g/ 8 oz flour, unless advised to the contrary.

Cobs

These are an excellent substitute for bread. They are made in minutes and must be eaten fresh. They freeze well.

225 g/8 oz self-raising flour
pinch salt
25 g/1 oz butter or margarine
approximately 150 ml/¼ pint milk

Preheat the oven to 230°C/450°F, Gas Mark 8. Lightly grease a baking tray. Sift the flour and salt into a bowl. Rub in the butter or margarine. Add enough milk to make a soft binding consistency – the mixture must not be too stiff, but rather sticky. Divide the dough into 10 to 12 portions and roll into balls with floured hands. Place on the baking tray and cook for 10 minutes, or until they feel firm, are golden brown in colour and crisp. ***Makes 10 to 12***

Gems

These small sweet scones are famous in Australia where they were baked in special gem irons, much cherished by their owners. Deep patty tins can be used instead. Both the Gems and Rusks are delicious with butter and jam or cheese. Serve when fresh. Both freeze well.

> 110 g/4 oz self-raising flour
> pinch salt
> 40 g/1½ oz butter
> 40 g/1½ oz caster sugar
> 1 egg – size 2 or 3
> 120 ml/4 fl oz milk

Preheat the oven to 200°C/400°F, Gas Mark 6. Grease 12 Gem irons or deep patty tins. Place in the oven to become very hot. Sift the flour and salt. Cream the butter and sugar until soft and light, beat the egg with the milk. Fold into the creamed mixture together with the flour.

   Spoon into the hot irons or tins and bake for 10 minutes, or until well-risen and firm. *Makes 12*

Suffolk Rusks

> 225 g/8 oz self-raising flour
> pinch salt
> 40 g/1½ oz butter or margarine
> 1 tablespoon caster sugar, optional
> 150 ml/¼ pint milk

Preheat the oven to 200°C/400°F, Gas Mark 6. Sift the flour and salt, rub in the butter or margarine, add the sugar. Blend with enough milk to make a soft rolling consistency. Roll out to 2 cm/¾ inch in thickness. Cut into 12 rounds. Put on an ungreased baking tray; bake for 8 minutes, or until firm enough to handle. Remove from the oven, lower the heat to 180°C/350°F, Gas Mark 4. Cut each round in half horizontally. Place the cut side downwards on to baking trays. Bake for 10 minutes, or until golden brown and crisp. *Makes 24*

Apricot and Walnut Loaf

This is a good basic recipe for a teabread and it keeps well. If freezing the loaf, slice it first and put pieces of greaseproof or waxed paper between the slices. This means you can remove as many as you need at a time.

By using tenderized, ready-to-eat apricots you omit the need for pre-soaking the fruit. Ordinary dried apricots should be soaked for 12 hours in the liquid given in the recipe below. In this case, still follow the proportions given in the recipe below.

> 175 g/6 oz dried tenderized apricots
> 75 g/3 oz butter or margarine
> 225 ml/7½ fl oz water or orange or apple juice
> 1 tablespoon lemon juice
> 350 g/12 oz self-raising flour
> 100 g/4 oz caster or light brown sugar
> 2 eggs – size 1 or 2
> 75 g/3 oz walnuts

Preheat the oven to 180°C/350°F, Gas Mark 4. Grease and flour, or line a 900 g/2 lb loaf tin. Cut the apricots into small pieces and put into a large bowl. Melt the butter or margarine and add the hot fat to the apricots – this helps to soften them. Pour in the cold water or fruit juice. Stir in the lemon juice, flour and sugar, then add the well-beaten eggs. Chop the walnuts and add to the other ingredients.

Spoon into the prepared tin. Bake for 30 minutes, reduce the oven heat to 160°C/325°F, Gas Mark 3 and bake for a further 1 hour, or until firm to the touch. Turn out and store for 24 hours before cutting. Slice thinly and serve with butter. *Makes 1 loaf*

To make a change
Cherry and Apricot Loaf: Chop 75 g/3 oz glacé cherries, mix with the flour and add to the mixture, as in the recipe above.
Date Loaf: Use 350 g/12 oz chopped stoned dates instead of apricots. Put into a large bowl, add 225 ml/7½ fl oz boiling water and the 75 g/3 oz melted fat. When cool proceed as in the recipe above.
Oatmeal Loaf: Omit 100 g/4 oz flour; add 100 g/4 oz rolled (porridge) oats. Sift 1 level teaspoon baking powder with the self-raising flour.

Melting Moments

Most biscuits, like those on this page, store well in an airtight tin. If, after cooking, you find the biscuits are not sufficiently crisp, bake again for a few minutes. The word 'biscuit' means 'twice-baked'.

110 g/4 oz butter or hard margarine
75 g/3 oz caster sugar
few drops vanilla essence
1 egg yolk
150 g/5 oz self-raising flour
To coat the biscuits:
approximately 25 g/1 oz cornflakes

Preheat the oven to 180°C/350°F, Gas Mark 4. Lightly grease 2 baking trays. Cream the butter or margarine, sugar and essence until soft and light. Beat in the egg yolk, then the flour. Divide into 18 to 20 small pieces. Roll into balls. If the dough is soft, chill for a short time. Crush the cornflakes and coat the balls. Place on the baking trays, allowing room for them to spread. Bake for 15 to 18 minutes, or until firm and golden. Cool on baking trays. *Makes 18 to 20*

Easter Biscuits

150 g/5 oz butter
110 g/4 oz caster sugar
grated zest of 1 lemon
225 g/8 oz plain flour
pinch mixed spice
1 egg yolk
75 g/3 oz currants

Preheat the oven and prepare baking trays as above. Cream the butter, sugar and lemon zest until soft. Sift the flour and spice and add to the creamed mixture with the egg yolk and currants. Mix well. Chill if necessary. Roll out until 0.5 cm/¼ inch in thickness and cut into rounds. Place on trays and bake for 12 minutes or until firm. *Makes about 18*

Moroccan Almond Macaroons

The almond-flavoured biscuits found in Morocco take a number of forms. The first recipe uses proportions similar to those in almond macaroons, but a subtle difference is made by heating the ground almonds. Rice paper is not used as a base, but could be if desired.

All these biscuits spread slightly when cooking, so allow space for this on the baking tray.

> 110 g/4 oz icing sugar
> 110 g/4 oz ground almonds
> ½ teaspoon lemon zest, optional
> pinch ground cinnamon, optional
> 2 egg whites from size 1 or 2 eggs
> *To decorate:*
> few blanched almonds

Preheat the oven to 180°C/350°F, Gas Mark 4. Place baking parchment or lightly greased greaseproof paper on baking trays. Sift the icing sugar into a saucepan. Add the ground almonds, lemon zest and cinnamon. Stir over a low heat for a few minutes, until the mixture forms a paste. Allow to cool. Whisk the egg whites until they just hold a shape. Blend with the almond mixture. Cut the blanched almonds into strips.

Either put small spoonfuls, or pipe the mixture into 3.5 cm/1½ inch rounds, on to the trays. Insert the almonds into the top of the biscuits. Bake for 15 minutes, or until just firm. Do not allow the biscuits to become too brown. *Makes about 15*

To make a change

Almond Biscuits: Use 1 whole egg instead of the egg whites. Blend with 225 g/8 oz ground almonds, 175 g/6 oz sifted icing sugar, the grated zest from 1 large lemon and a good pinch of ground cinnamon. Roll into 24 balls, place on the prepared trays. Top with whole blanched almonds. Bake as the recipe above. *Makes about 24*

Italian Amaretti Biscuits: Blend 200 g/7 oz caster sugar, 1 level tablespoon ground rice, 110 g/4 oz ground almonds, 2 unwhisked egg whites and a few drops of almond essence. Put very small spoonfuls, or pipe into 2.5 cm/1 inch rounds, on to the lined trays. Bake as the first recipe until pale golden brown. *Makes about 30*

Kransekake

This Norwegian, almond-flavoured Garland Cake is made from a firm biscuit mixture formed into rings. These are assembled to make a pyramid shape, then decorated with glacé icing. The amounts below give a rather modest-sized cake. For a special occasion you will need to increase these to give a far higher and more impressive pyramid. In Norway this is primarily a cake for weddings, but it can be served for any special occasion.

While ready-ground almonds can be used, you'll achieve a more interesting flavour if you grind almonds in their skins.

> 300 g/10 oz unblanched almonds
> 300 g/10 oz icing sugar
> 25 g/1 oz plain flour
> 2 egg whites
> *For rolling:*
> little icing sugar
> *For the glacé icing:*
> 150 g/5 oz icing sugar
> 1 to 1¼ tablespoons water

Grind the almonds in a food processor or liquidizer (blender). Sift the icing sugar and blend with the almonds, then put into the food processor or liquidizer once more to give a very fine and perfectly blended mixture. Put into a bowl, add the flour and the unwhisked egg whites. Mix together then cover for 24 hours. This makes the mixture easier to handle.

Dust a working surface with sifted icing sugar. Form pieces of the dough into finger-thick sausage shapes then cut into various lengths. The top ring would be formed from a piece about 2 cm/¾ inch long and each lower ring should be slightly longer, so you can make a well-graduated pyramid.

Preheat the oven to 220°C/425°F, Gas Mark 7. Line baking trays with greased greaseproof paper or baking parchment. Place the rings on these. Bake for 7 minutes only. The mixture will be firm on the outside but still beautifully soft in the centre. Cool, and assemble into the pyramid on the serving dish or cake board.

For the glacé icing: Sift the icing sugar and blend with the water to give a flowing consistency. Put into an icing bag with a fine, writing pipe and decorate each ring with lines of icing. ***Makes one cake***

Florentines

Florentines are delicious biscuits and can be formed into midget-sized rounds and served as *petits fours*. The timing of the baking is particularly important. When cooked and cold, store in an airtight tin away from other biscuits. They keep for about a week.

> 100 g/4 oz blanched almonds
> 50 g/2 oz candied peel
> 25 g/1 oz glacé cherries
> 25 g/1 oz sultanas
> 75 g/3 oz unsalted butter
> 75 g/3 oz caster sugar
> 1 level tablespoon plain flour
> 1 tablespoon double cream
> *To coat the biscuits:*
> 175 g/6 oz plain chocolate

Grease several baking trays or, better still, line them with baking parchment. Preheat the oven to 180°C/350°F, Gas Mark 4.

Cut the almonds into neat slivers (strips). Chop the peel, cherries and sultanas into small pieces. Melt the butter and sugar in a saucepan or a basin in the microwave. Add the prepared nuts and fruits, then beat in the flour and cream.

Put 14 to 18 small spoonfuls of the mixture on to the parchment, allowing plenty of room for the biscuits to spread. If making *petits fours,* make about 40 miniature rounds of the mixture. Bake for 6 to 10 minutes, depending upon the size, until golden brown. Check the cooking carefully, for these biscuits burn easily. Remove from the oven and gently pull the edges of the biscuits inwards to neaten the shape. Leave on the parchment until cold. Remove, and turn upside down.

Melt the chocolate over hot, but not boiling, water or in the microwave. Cool slightly so that the chocolate spreads easily. Place the biscuits with the flat base uppermost on a wire cooling tray with a dish underneath to catch any drips of chocolate. Spread a layer of chocolate over the base of the biscuits. Allow this to set then turn over so the fruity side is uppermost. ***Makes 14 to 18***

Brandy Snaps

I have included this recipe because as well as producing a delicious, biscuit-like cake to serve with tea or coffee, the crisp mixture is very useful as a container for desserts such as ice cream. The rolling, or moulding, of the mixture is not difficult providing you time the baking carefully. Do not try and cook too many biscuits at the same time. If you make them in batches you will be able to roll, or mould, one batch before the next ones come out of the oven.

Store in an airtight tin, away from other biscuits. They keep for several weeks.

> **50 g/2 oz unsalted butter**
> **50 g/2 oz caster sugar**
> **2 level tablespoons golden syrup**
> **50 g/2 oz plain flour, less 1 level teaspoon**
> **½ teaspoon ground ginger, optional**

Grease and flour several baking trays or line these with baking parchment. Preheat the oven to 180°C/350°F, Gas Mark 4.

Grease the handles of several wooden spoons or, if you want to make basket-shaped containers for desserts, grease small upturned patty or muffin tins.

Put the butter, sugar and syrup into a saucepan. Stir over the heat until just melted. Sift the flour and ginger and fold into the mixture. Put 10 to 12 small spoonfuls of the mixture on to the trays, allowing plenty of room for the mixture to spread. Put the first tray into the oven and bake for 7 to 10 minutes or until golden brown. Bring out of the oven, cool for 1 or 2 minutes, or until you can remove the first biscuit with a palette knife. Roll the biscuit around the handle of the wooden spoon, or press over the tin. Continue like this with the rest of the biscuits. You can remove them from the spoon handle, or the tin, after a few minutes, for they set rapidly. Place on a wire cooling tray.

Continue until all the biscuits are baked and shaped.   *Makes 10 to 12*

To make a change
Omit the ginger. Flavour the mixture with the grated zest of ½ a lemon. Add 1 teaspoon brandy (in this case use the full 50 g/2 oz of flour).
Honey Snaps: Use thin honey instead of golden syrup. Flavour with the lemon zest and brandy, as above.

Meringues

These are some of the most useful of all sweet biscuit-like cakes. They can be served plain or sandwiched together with whipped cream for teatime or for a dessert. They are delicious filled with ice cream.

A light sponge, such as the Blötkake, on page 184, becomes a more interesting gateau if the sides are decorated with tiny meringues. The ultimate meringue is a Pavlova. This is perfect for special occasions.

Rather than always making plain meringues, try experimenting with various flavourings. Do not put the filling into meringues until just before serving: if cream is added too soon it softens them. If stored in an airtight tin, meringues keep well for weeks. They can be frozen, but soften quickly after defrosting. A Pavlova, with its soft centre, is better served within a day of making, or stored in the freezer.

> **2 egg whites**
> **few drops vanilla essence,** *see note* **below**
> **110 g/4 oz caster or use half sifted icing sugar**
> **and half caster sugar**

Brush one or more baking trays with a few drops of oil, or use non-stick trays or line trays with baking parchment. Preheat the oven to 90 to 110°C/ 200 to 225°F, Gas Mark S or ¼. Slightly quicker baking sets the outside and gives a stickier centre, in which case set the oven to 110 to 120°C/225 to 250°F, Gas Mark ½ to 1.

Put the egg whites and essence into a large bowl. Whisk by hand or with an electric mixer until stiff; you should be able to turn the bowl upside down without the mixture falling out. Do not whisk until the egg whites are dry and crumbly. Gradually beat in half the sugar(s) and then fold in the remainder. Spoon or pipe into the desired shape and size on the prepared trays. The mixture makes 12 medium or 24 small, or finger-shaped meringues, or 60 very small ones (suitable for small children).

Bake for 1 to 1¼ hours for very tiny meringues and up to 2½ to 3 hours for medium ones. When cooked, the meringues lift easily from the trays. If using the hotter temperatures, the shorter baking times should be adequate. Cool, then store until ready to use. ***Makes 12 to 60***

Note: Vanilla essence will do, but the best flavour is obtained with vanilla pods. Halve one or more of these and place into a jar of sugar. Leave until the sugar is well-flavoured. Weigh out the amount required in the recipe. If you use vanilla-flavoured sugar, omit the vanilla essence.

Pavlova

Pavlova is believed to have been a favourite of Anna Pavlova, the ballerina.

The meringue should be crisp on the outside but soft, rather like a light-textured marshmallow, inside. *See note* at the bottom of the page.

> **4 egg whites**
> **225 g/8 oz caster sugar, or** *see* **Flavourings for**
> **Meringues**
> **1½ level teaspoons cornflour**
> **1½ teaspoons white vinegar**
> **1 teaspoon vanilla essence, or** *see* **note,**
>   **under Meringues, page 175**

Prepare the baking trays as for Meringues. Make a circle of the required size on the baking parchment. The secret of a Pavlova with the texture described above is to put the meringue into an oven preheated to a higher temperature, then *immediately* alter this to the lower setting. As the heat drops in a gas oven quickly a higher setting can be used than in an electric oven. Preheat an electric oven to 180°C/350°F then lower to 150°C/300°F; preheat a gas oven to Mark 7 then lower to Mark 2.

Whisk the whites as under Meringues. Blend the sugar and cornflour; beat into the egg whites a tablespoon at a time. Fold the vinegar and essence into the meringue. Spoon or pipe into a flan shape. Place in the preheated oven, as described above; lower the heat and bake for approximately 50 minutes, or until crisp on the outside and pale beige colour. Cool in the oven with the heat turned off, then fill.

Fillings for a Pavlova: Whipped cream, blended with passion fruit, or other fruit purée or whole fruit, such as raspberries, strawberries or mixed fruits, or lemon curd (lemon cheese) or ice cream and fruit.

Flavourings for Meringues: The quantities are for 2 egg whites, as page 175

Chocolate Meringues: Sift 1 level tablespoon cocoa powder or 2 level tablespoons chocolate powder into the sugar.

Coconut Meringues: Add 50 g/2 oz desiccated coconut to the sugar.

Coffee Meringues: Add 1½ level teaspoons instant coffee to the sugar.

Nut Meringues: Add 50 g/2 oz finely chopped hazelnuts, toasted ground almonds or walnuts to the sugar.

Note: For a crisp texture throughout, omit the vinegar and cornflour, make the meringue as described for Meringues, shape as Pavlova but bake as for Meringues for 3 to 4 hours.

Angel Cake

This cake really is 'as light as a feather', because it is based on whisked egg whites. It makes an excellent accompaniment to fruits of various kinds.

American experts have conducted many experiments into the best ways to perfect the cake. The general consensus of opinion is that the egg whites should be about 3 days old and the oven heat moderate.

> **8 egg whites – size 1 or 2 eggs, or 9 egg whites –**
>   **size 3 eggs**
> **110 g/4 oz self-raising flour**
> **pinch salt**
> **175 g/6 oz caster sugar**
> **½ level teaspoon cream of tartar**
> **1 tablespoon lemon juice or water**
> *To decorate:*
> **little icing sugar**
> **glacé cherries**

Use a 23 cm/9 inch ring tin. This should have straight sides and it should *not* be greased. Preheat the oven to 180°C/350°F, Gas Mark 4.

Put the eggs into the bowl and, if they come from the refrigerator, leave at room temperature for 1 hour. Sift the flour at least twice and leave on a plate at room temperature. This lightens it. Whisk the egg whites until foamy, but do not overbeat at any stage. Blend in the salt and just 1 tablespoon of the sugar. Continue whisking until nearly stiff, then fold in another tablespoon sugar and the cream of tartar.

Whisk until the egg whites form soft peaks. Blend the sugar and flour and gradually fold this mixture, with the lemon juice or water, into the whites. Spoon into the tin. Bake for 50 minutes to 1 hour or until firm to a gentle touch.

Invert the cake on to a milk bottle, or similar shape, so this is under the hole in the middle of the tin. The cake itself should not touch the bottle. Do *not* put the cake on to a wire cooling tray. When the cake is quite cold and firm, gently shake the tin and the cake will drop out. Top with sifted icing sugar and cherries.   *Serves 8*

Flavourings for Angel Cake: Add ½ teaspoon vanilla or almond essence.
Chocolate Angel Cake: Sift 15 g/½ oz cocoa powder with 85 g/3½ oz flour.
Coffee Angel Cake: Use very strong coffee instead of lemon juice or water.
Spiced Angel Cake: Sift 1 teaspoon ground cinnamon with the flour.

Linzertorte

The texture of this filled flan is half-way between a biscuit and a cake. It is delicious with tea or coffee, or served as a dessert. Fresh raspberries are best but jam is a good alternative.

> 175 g/6 oz butter or margarine
> 75 g/3 oz caster sugar
> finely grated zest of 1 lemon
> 1 egg – size 1 or 2
> 225 g/8 oz plain flour sifted with ½ level
>   teaspoon baking powder
> ½ teaspoon ground cinnamon
> 50 g/2 oz ground nuts – almonds, hazelnuts or
>   walnuts, *see* method
> *For the filling:*
> 450 g/1 lb raspberries with sugar to taste or
>   approximately 300 g/10 oz raspberry jam
> 2 tablespoons redcurrant jelly
> little icing sugar

Lightly grease a 20 cm/8 inch fluted or plain flan ring. Place this on an upturned baking tray, or use a flan tin. Preheat the oven to 180 to 190°C/350° to 375°F, Gas Mark 4 to 5. Choose the lower setting if your oven is inclined to be fierce.

Cream the butter or margarine with the sugar and lemon zest until soft. Beat in the egg. Sift the flour and baking powder with the cinnamon and fold into the creamed mixture with the nuts. Buy these already ground or liquidize or process whole nuts. Leave the skins on the nuts if possible, for these give a more interesting flavour to the dough. Do not over-process the nuts, or they will become sticky.

Knead the dough. If too soft to handle, wrap and chill for a time. Roll out two-thirds of the dough on a lightly floured board and line the flan. Roll out the remaining dough; cut into strips about 0.5 cm/¼ inch wide. Mash the raspberries with a little sugar and put into the flan – or use the jam. Arrange the strips in a lattice over the fruit or jam. Bake for 30 to 35 minutes, or until firm. Place foil over the fruit or jam if becoming over-cooked. Melt the redcurrant jelly, brush over the filling. Serve warm or cold. Dust with sifted icing sugar just before serving.   ***Serves 6***

Dutch Apple Cake

This is another cake which, like Linzertorte on page 178, can be eaten for tea, with coffee, or as a dessert. It is at its best freshly made; but as it freezes extremely well it is worthwhile making the fairly large amount given in the recipe and freezing any surplus. Choose dessert apples that cook well and keep their shape during baking – Cox's Orange Pippin or Granny Smith are good varieties.

150 g/5 oz butter or margarine
150 g/5 oz caster sugar
grated zest of 1 lemon
2 eggs – size 1 or 2
300 g/10 oz self-raising flour
little milk
For the topping:
675 g/1½ lb dessert apples
1½ tablespoons lemon juice
25 g/1 oz icing sugar
4 tablespoons apricot jam

Line a Swiss roll tin approximately 30 x 23 cm/12 x 9 inches with greased greaseproof or waxed paper, or baking parchment. Preheat the oven to 190°C/375°F, Gas Mark 5. Cream the butter or margarine, sugar and lemon zest until soft and light. Whisk the eggs, then gradually beat into the creamed mixture. Stir in the flour, mix thoroughly, then add sufficient milk to make a sticky consistency, i.e. one that drops from a spoon when shaken vigorously – do not make the mixture too wet.

Spread the cake mixture over the paper or parchment. Peel and slice the apples, and arrange in neat lines on the dough; keep away from the side edges, for that allows these to rise and form a good border. Sprinkle the apples with the lemon juice and sift the icing sugar over the top.

Bake for 40 minutes or until the apples are tender and the cake is golden in colour; reduce the heat slightly when the cake has risen well. Remove from the tin. Warm, and then sieve the jam; brush over the apples. Cut into neat slices and serve warm or cold   *Serves 6 to 8*

To make a change
Dutch Cherry Cake: Use stoned dessert cherries instead of apples and glaze the cooked fruit with melted redcurrant jelly in place of apricot jam.

Coconut Pyramids

These are delicious teatime treats. If the mixture is a little dry, add a few drops of milk or, better still, use cream. If too moist then add a little more coconut.

2 egg whites from size 1 or 2 eggs
175 g/6 oz desiccated coconut
½ level tablespoon cornflour
75 to 100 g/3 to 4 oz caster sugar
For base of pyramids:
rice paper

Preheat the oven to 160°C/325°F, Gas Mark 3. Place rice paper on one or two baking trays. If not available lightly grease the tray(s).

Whisk the egg whites until they are almost stiff, then add the rest of the ingredients. Form into 12 medium or 18 tiny pyramid shapes. Place on the tray(s). Bake for 10 minutes, or until the tips are golden-brown. Store apart from other cakes in an airtight tin.   ***Makes 12 to 18***

Lamingtons

These Australian cakes and the traditional British Madeleines on page 181 are based on light cake mixtures, made by the creaming method. If using soft margarine, put all the ingredients for the cakes into the bowl together and beat these until smooth.

175 g/6 oz butter or margarine
175 g/6 oz caster sugar
3 eggs – size 1 or 2
175 g/6 oz self-raising flour
To coat the cakes:
225 g/8 oz icing sugar
25 g/1 oz cocoa powder
2 tablespoons water
few drops vanilla essence
15 g/½ oz butter
75 g/3 oz desiccated coconut

Preheat the oven to 180°C/350°F, Gas Mark 4. Grease and flour, or line a 20 cm/8 inch square tin. Cream the butter or margarine and sugar until soft and light. Beat the eggs; gradually beat into the creamed mixture. Fold in the flour. Spoon the mixture into the tin. Smooth flat on top. Bake for 20 to 25 minutes. To test if cooked, press in the centre with your forefinger: the cake should be firm to the touch. Turn out on to a wire cooling tray. When cold cut into 16 squares.

Sift the icing sugar with the cocoa powder. Put into a saucepan with the water, vanilla essence and butter. Stir over a low heat until a flowing consistency. Put the coconut on to a large sheet of greaseproof paper or a large dish.

Insert a a fine skewer into the first square of cake. Dip in the warm icing until evenly and thinly coated. Drop into the coconut and turn until evenly covered. Repeat this process with the rest of the squares. Stand for several hours for the coating to harden. *Makes 16*

Madeleines

110 g/4 oz butter or margarine
110 g/4 oz caster sugar
2 eggs – size 1 or 2
110 g/4 oz self-raising flour
To coat the cakes:
3 to 4 tablespoons raspberry jam
50 g/2 oz desiccated coconut
6 to 8 glacé cherries
24 to 32 small angelica leaves

Preheat the oven to 200°C/400°F, Gas Mark 6. Grease and lightly flour 12 to 16 dariole (castle pudding) tins.

Cream the butter or margarine and sugar until soft and light. Add the beaten eggs and fold in the flour. Half-fill the tins. Bake the cakes for 10 to 12 minutes, or until firm. Turn out and cool.

Sieve and warm the jam. Place the coconut on a large dish. Insert a fine skewer or toothpick into the base of the first cake. Hold the end of it. Brush the sides and base of the cake with jam. Roll in the coconut. Repeat with all the cakes. Halve the cherries, place on the cakes with the angelica leaves. *Makes 12 to 16*

Lemon Cheesecake

Allow baked cheesecakes to cool in the oven, with the heat turned off. Leave the door just ajar in an electric oven. This prevents the cake wrinkling. This cheesecake freezes well.

For the base of the cheesecake:
175 g/6 oz digestive biscuits
85 g/3 oz butter
50 g/2 oz caster sugar
For the filling:
50 g/2 oz butter
50 g/2 oz caster sugar
1 teaspoon finely grated lemon zest
2 eggs – size 1 or 2
350 g/12 oz cream or curd cheese
2 tablespoons lemon juice
2 tablespoons double cream
To decorate:
thin strips of lemon zest
150 ml/¼ pint double cream

Grease a 20 cm/8 inch cake tin with a loose base. Preheat the oven to 150°C/ 300°F, Gas Mark 2. Crush the biscuits, melt the butter. Blend with the biscuit crumbs and sugar. Press into the base of the tin.

Cream the butter, sugar and lemon zest until soft and light. Whisk the eggs and gradually beat into the butter mixture. Add the cheese, then the lemon juice and cream. Mix well and spoon over the base.

Bake for 1¼ hours, or until firm. Allow to cool in the tin, then remove the cake by pushing the base of the tin upwards with a large jug, or other utensil, so the cake is supported but the tin sides fall away. Lift the cake from the base with a thin fish slice.

Simmer the lemon zest in water for 5 minutes; drain and dry. Whip the cream and pipe on the cheesecake. Top with the lemon strips.   **Serves 6**

To make a change
Fruit Cheesecake: Add 175 g/6 oz drained, chopped canned pineapple, apricots or mangoes and omit the cream. Use fruit syrup in place of lemon juice. Decorate the top with whipped cream and fruit.

Sachertorte

If filled with a thick apricot purée rather than with jam, this deliciously rich Austrian chocolate cake can be served for a dessert. Make quite sure that the chocolate for the cake and for the icing is not over-heated, or it will lose its moist texture and consistency, as well as its shine. This cake keeps for several days and it freezes well.

> **150 g/5 oz plain chocolate**
> **1 tablespoon water**
> **150 g/5 oz butter or margarine**
> **150 g/5 oz icing sugar**
> **5 eggs – size 1**
> **150 g/5 oz plain flour sifted with 1 teaspoon**
>   **baking powder**
> **1 egg white – size 1 egg**
> *To fill and coat:*
> **3 to 6 tablespoons apricot jam,** *see* **method**
> **175 g/6 oz plain chocolate**
> **1 tablespoon water**
> **2 drops olive oil**

Preheat the oven to 150°C/300°F, Gas Mark 2. Line a 23 cm/9 inch cake tin with greased greaseproof paper or baking parchment.

For the cake: Break the chocolate into pieces. Put into a bowl with the water and melt over hot, but not boiling, water, or in the microwave. Cool, then add the butter or margarine. Sift the icing sugar into the bowl and cream until soft and light. Separate the eggs. Gradually beat the yolks into the chocolate mixture, then fold in the flour and baking powder. Whisk the 6 egg whites until just stiff, but not too dry and crumbly. Fold into the cake ingredients. Spoon into the tin and bake for 50 to 60 minutes, or until firm to the touch. Cool in the tin for 3 minutes, then turn out on to a wire cooling tray and remove the paper or parchment.

To fill and coat: The cake is so rich that it is not essential to split and fill this with jam. If you do want to do this, you will need the 6 tablespoons apricot jam. Sieve the jam and coat the top of the cake with 3 tablespoons. Break the chocolate into pieces and melt, as above, adding the water and oil. Cool sufficiently to make a spreading consistency and carefully spread over the jam topping. Allow to set.　　　　　　　　*Makes one cake*

183

Blötkake

This Norwegian layer cake is made by the whisking method of mixing. Baking powder is not strictly necessary, since air has been incorporated by whisking, but I include it for it ensures that the sponge rises well.

> 4 eggs – size 1 or 2
> 175 g/6 oz caster sugar
> 85 g/3 oz self-raising flour or plain or potato
>   flour sifted with 1 level teaspoon baking
>   powder

Grease and flour a 20 to 23 cm/8 to 9 inch cake tin, or line with baking parchment. Preheat the oven to 180°C/350°F, Gas Mark 4.

Separate the eggs. Beat the yolks well with half the sugar until thick and creamy. Whisk the egg whites until stiff, and gradually fold in the remaining sugar. Blend the yolks into the whites, then gradually fold in the very well sifted flour, or flour and baking powder.

Spoon into the tin; bake for 35 to 40 minutes or until firm to a gentle touch. Cool for a few minutes in the tin, then place on to a wire cooling tray, top side uppermost. Allow to become cold. Cut the sponge into layers and fill with preserves or with whipped cream and fruit. Decorate the top with more whipped cream and fruit.   ***Makes one cake***

To make a change
Swiss Roll: Line a 30 x 23 cm/12 x 9 inch Swiss roll tin with greased greaseproof paper or baking parchment. Preheat the oven to 190°C/375°F, Gas Mark 5. Sprinkle a sheet of greaseproof paper with caster sugar. Whisk 3 eggs – size 1 or 2 – with 110 g/4 oz caster sugar until thick and creamy. Fold in 85 g/3 oz well sifted self-raising or plain flour with baking powder (*see* introduction, above). Spoon into the prepared tin and bake for 8 to 10 minutes, or until firm to a gentle touch.

Meanwhile warm, but do not overheat, about 6 tablespoons jam. Turn the sponge on to the sugared paper, with one of the shorter ends nearest to you. Remove the baking paper or parchment, spread the sponge with the jam and roll firmly.
Hazelnut Roulade: Follow the Swiss Roll recipe, but use 85 g/3 oz finely chopped hazelnuts instead of flour; omit baking powder. When cooked, roll with greaseproof paper inside. Cool and unroll. Fill with whipped cream and jam, then roll up again. Other nuts could be used instead.

Frangipane Tartlets

The pastry given in this recipe is ideal for any sweet tarts. Frangipane filling takes time to make but it is delicious.

For the Frangipane filling:
1 level tablespoon cornflour
225 ml/7½ fl oz single cream or milk
2 eggs
25 to 50 g/1 to 2 oz caster sugar, *see* method
50 g/2 oz ground almonds or macaroon crumbs
For the sweet pastry:
175 g/6 oz plain flour
85 g/3 oz butter or hard margarine
50 g/2 oz caster sugar
1 egg yolk, plus few drops of water
To fill the tartlet cases:
2 tablespoons apricot jam

Blend the cornflour with the cream or milk and pour into a saucepan. Stir over a low heat until a firm mixture; remove from the heat. Beat the eggs and blend with the thick sauce. Cook slowly, stirring all the time until thick again. Add the sugar. Use the smaller amount with macaroon crumbs. Stir in the ground almonds or cake crumbs. Leave until cold.

Sift the flour into a bowl and rub in the butter or margarine until the mixture is like fine breadcrumbs. Add the sugar, egg yolk and water to make a rolling consistency. Wrap and chill, then roll out and line 12 deep or 18 shallow patty tins. Preheat the oven to 200°C/400°F, Gas Mark 6.

Prick the base of the pastry cases. Bake for 5 minutes in the oven. Lower the heat to 190°C/375°F, Gas Mark 5. Put a little jam into each pastry case. Add the Frangipane filling. Bake for a further 10 minutes, or until pastry and filling are firm. **Makes 12 to 18**

To make a change
Macaroon Tartlets: Make the pastry. Line the tartlet tins, then put in the jam. Lightly whisk 2 egg whites with a few drops of almond essence, add 110 g/4 oz ground almonds and 110 g/4 oz caster sugar. Spoon over the jam and bake for 20 minutes at 200°C/400°F, Gas Mark 6. Lower heat if necessary after 15 minutes if the filling is becoming too brown.

Christmas Cake - 1952

The recipe below is the one I demonstrated on BBC TV in 1952, when at long last the end of food rationing was within sight. Over the years I have added a few extra ingredients. The original cake recipe gave margarine, as butter was still in short supply. Use plain flour, with no baking powder. A cake mixture lightened with baking powder will not hold the fruit in position: this may sink during baking.

> 225 g/8 oz butter or margarine
> 225 g/8 oz moist dark brown sugar
> 1 level tablespoon golden syrup or black treacle
> finely grated rind of 1 lemon
> 4 eggs – size 1 or 2
> 4 tablespoons milk or sweet sherry or brandy
> 350 g/12 oz plain flour
> 1 teaspoon mixed spice
> ½ teaspoon ground cinnamon
> 110 g/4 oz glacé cherries
> 110 g/4 oz blanched almonds
> 110 g/4 oz mixed candied peel
> 900 g/2 lb mixed dried fruit, preferably
>   450 g/1 lb currants
>   225 g/8 oz sultanas
>   225 g/8 oz raisins

Line the base of a 23 cm/9 inch round or 20 cm/8 inch square tin with brown paper and then with greased greaseproof paper or baking parchment. Line the sides with paper or parchment. Tie a deep band of brown paper around the outside of the tin. It is worth taking time to prepare the tin, for this helps to keep the cake moist and prevent it over-browning. Preheat the oven to 160°C/325°F, Gas Mark 3.

Cream the butter or margarine with the sugar, golden syrup or treacle and the lemon zest until soft – do not overbeat the mixture. Beat the eggs with the milk, sherry or brandy. Sift the flour and spices. Blend the beaten egg mixture and flour alternately into the creamed ingredients. Chop the cherries, almonds and peel; mix with the dried fruits. Add these ingredients to the cake mixture and blend thoroughly. Spoon into the cake tin and smooth the mixture quite flat on top.

To bake the cake:

Press the top of the mixture with dampened knuckles; this helps to prevent the top becoming over-crisp and hard.

Bake for 1½ hours at 160°C/325°F, Gas Mark 3. This sets the outside of the cake quickly and keeps the cake moist. Reduce the heat to 140 or 150°C/275 or 300°F, Gas Mark 1 or 2, and bake for a further 2 hours. Use the lower temperature if your oven is inclined to be rather fierce. Baking times for large, rich cakes vary considerably *so test carefully*. A rich fruit cake is cooked when silent. If there is a faint humming sound the cake is not quite cooked. Allow to cool in the tin.

Remove the greaseproof paper or parchment; store in an airtight tin. This cake improves by being kept for at least 2 weeks before icing.

To make a change

Add the grated zest of an orange as well as the lemon zest.

Omit 50 g/2 oz flour and add the same amount of ground almonds; *or* use 5 eggs and only 2 tablespoons liquid. Prick the cake when cold and at intervals of 10 days and soak with sherry or brandy or rum.

For a richer cake: Use 300 g/10 oz of butter and 300 g/10 oz sugar with 550 g/1¼ lb currants, 300 g/10 oz sultanas and 300 g/10 oz raisins. This is sufficiently rich for a wedding cake. Increase baking time at 140°C/275°F, Gas Mark 1, by about 45 minutes, but test carefully. This cake is better kept for at least 3 weeks before icing.

For a small Christmas cake: Use half the quantities given on page 186. Bake in a 15 to 18 cm/6 to 7 inch round or 13 to 15 cm/5 to 6 inch square tin. Allow 1 hour at 160°C/325°F, Gas Mark 3 and a further 1¼ to 1½ hours at the lower setting, *see* above.

To decorate the cake:

Quantities are for the size of cake given on page 186.

Marzipan: Blend 400 g/14 oz ground almonds, a few drops of almond essence, 200 g/7 oz sifted icing sugar, 200 g/7 oz caster sugar. Bind with 2 to 3 egg yolks, or the whites if preferred. Brush the cake with sieved apricot jam. Roll out the marzipan on a sugared surface to make a round or square large enough to cover the cake. Put on the cake. Leave for 48 hours before coating with Royal Icing.

Royal Icing: Whisk 4 egg whites until frothy. Add 900 g/2 lb sifted icing sugar and 1 tablespoon lemon juice. Beat until white and glossy. If you prefer softer icing, add 2 teaspoons glycerine. This quantity makes enough to cover the cake and leaves some over for decoration.

Maids of Honour

It is thought that these tarts were made in the reign of King Henry VIII by Anne Boleyn's maids of honour to please this lady and the king.

pastry as Frangipane Tartlets, *see* page 185
  or 175 g/6 oz frozen puff pastry *see* note
For the filling:
175 g/6 oz cottage or low fat curd cheese
50 g/2 oz butter
50 g/2 oz caster sugar
½ teaspoon grated lemon zest
2 egg yolks or 1 egg – size 1 or 2
25 g/1 oz ground almonds or fine cake crumbs
2 teaspoons brandy or orange flower water

Preheat the oven to 200°C/400°F, Gas Mark 6. Roll out the pastry and line 12 to 18 patty tins. If using cottage cheese, sieve this. Cream the butter, sugar and lemon zest until soft and light. Beat the egg yolks or egg. Fold into the creamed mixture then add the cheese, ground almonds or cake crumbs and the brandy or orange flower water. Spoon into the pastry cases. Bake for 20 minutes. Reduce the heat slightly after 15 minutes if the filling is becoming too brown.

Note: If using puff pastry, bake for 10 minutes at 220°C/425°F, Gas Mark 7, then lower the heat to 160°C/325°F, Gas Mark 3 for 10 to 15 minutes. When cold, top the tartlets with glacé icing made by blending 110 g/4 oz sifted icing sugar with a little brandy or orange flower water.

Australian Icing

This icing is sold as sugar paste; but here is the recipe I use. Soften 11 g/½ oz (1 sachet) of gelatine in 3 tablespoons cold water or lemon juice. Put 120 ml/4 fl oz liquid glucose and 3 teaspoons glycerine into a saucepan. Heat, then add the softened gelatine. Stir over a low heat until dissolved. Remove from the heat; add 900 g/2 lb sifted icing sugar. Mix and knead until smooth. Roll out on a board coated with sifted icing sugar, until the size required. Cover the cake. Use the icing for moulding flowers, fruits, figures, etc. Use for Christmas, wedding or any rich cakes.

Index